Moss, Marshes & Memorable Meals

Highlighting Histor

Isle of Hope United Methodist Women

First Printing   August, 2006

Copies of *Moss, Marshes & Memorable Meals* may be obtained by contacting the Isle of Hope United Methodist Women at 912-355-8527, by using the order forms provided in the back of this edition, or at the address provided below.

Isle of Hope United Methodist Women
412 Parkersburg Road
Savannah, GA 31406

ISBN: 0-9786020-0-5

About the Artist

Chip Goldsmith is a native Savannahian who was born and raised on The Isle of Hope. A self-taught artist, Chip's paintings reflect his passion for life in the low country. He practices Neurotology at The Georgia Ear Institute in Savannah, where he founded The International Center for Otologic Training (ICOT). He currently resides on the Isle of Hope with his wife, Ruth; his three sons Miles, David, and Ben; three dogs, daVinci, Bear, and Twiggy; and two cats, Ziggy and Pete.
www.lowcountrywatercolors.com
912-350-5035

WIMMER
COOKBOOKS

A CONSOLIDATED GRAPHICS COMPANY

800.548.2537   wimmerco.com

Table of Contents

An Island Church

The Isle of Hope United Methodist Church began as a mission outreach in the 1830s, but it wasn't until 1841 that Elijah Day was appointed to serve as its first pastor. Originally, it was located across the causeway from the Isle of Hope in the area known as Sandfly. The church was formally organized in 1851, and in 1859, a new sanctuary was built at the current location on land donated by Dr. Stephen Dupon.

During the War Between the States, the church was used as a hospital for Confederate soldiers, many of whom were young volunteers from Effingham County. The original pews are still being used and some have initials carved by the soldiers during their recuperation. Iron crosses in the adjacent graveyard represent the thirty-five young soldiers who are buried there. Later, when Sherman's men were stationed at the church, they used the sanctuary as a camp and took the bell from the steeple to melt for cannon balls.

Isle of Hope remained a country church until the late 1940s when the island became more densely populated. The first full-time pastor was appointed in 1950. In 1959, the church building was relocated under the oaks, a short distance back from its initial location at the edge of the Parkersburg Road. In 1984, as the sanctuary was being enlarged, it burned to the ground. The building was quickly rebuilt using the original design. Fortunately, the original pews, lighting fixtures, pulpit and altar rail were in storage at the time of the fire and now grace the church. The wooden cross over the altar was built by church members from charred timbers which survived the fire.

In the early 1900s, the Ladies Aid Society was formed to support the church. The women had meager resources but they gave generously of their time, talents and prayers. They pieced quilt coverlets which they sold and also sponsored chicken suppers and bazaars to raise money for missions, improvements and repairs to the building.

Today the Isle of Hope United Methodist Church has an active congregation of over 2500 members. Its emphasis remains on Christian care for the Savannah community and on missions throughout the United States and the world. It is known for its generosity in support of Savannah organizations and individuals involved in caring for spiritual, physical and emotional needs and for reaching out to other parts of the world in service and ministry.

Acknowledgments

Co-Chair
Nancy Hartmann   Linda Martin

Section Chairs
Caryn Andrews   Heather Batchelor
Annette Daniel   Karen Daniel
Michelle Dunn   Sandra Harn
Margaret Hughes   Linda Meyer
Nancy Montford   Ann Sherrill
Marjo Zelinsky

Support
Pat Biggerstaff   Lynn Hagan
Jeanette Mayo   Gail Murphy
Dianna Phillips

Paintings
Chip Goldsmith

Narrative and Photographic Contributors
Lewis Brinson   Ray Kitchens
Bobbie Norris   Lisa Sharpley

United Methodist Women President
Joan Broerman

No claim is made as to originality of these recipes. They have been tried, sometimes altered, adapted, adopted and enjoyed. Recipes in this book include recipes from The Day on the Island Cookbook, The New Day on the Island Cookbook and Under the Oaks, previous Isle of Hope cookbooks.

Contributors List
United Methodist Women, of The Isle of Hope United Methodist Church, wish to express their deep appreciation to the following members and friends of our church who so generously contributed their recipes to make this cookbook possible. We regret we were unable to publish all recipes due to similarity or availability of space. To anyone whose name we have inadvertently omitted, please accept our sincere apology.

Contributors

Andrews, Barbara
Andrews, Caryn
Arnold, Grace
Barnes, Betty
Beall, Carla
Beals, Alan
Beals, Sandi
Beason, Carole
Biggerstaff, Pat
Binford, Sue
Brinson, Judy
Broerman, Joan
Broerman, Kimberly
Brook, Joyce
Bryan, Suzanne Clary
Buck, Marilyn
Burgess, Dori
Borges, Katie
Burbank, Ellie
Byrd, Florence
Coker, Elinor
Cook, Brenda
Curlee, Gray
Curlee, Phyllis
Daniel, Annette
Daniel, Karen
Davenport, Jan
Davis, Dotty
Davis, Suzanne
Dewberry, Dotsie
Dimond, Julie
Dunn, Ken
Edgerton, Patricia
Falligant, Carol
Floyd, Kim
Fountain, Amy Louise
Franklin, Betsy
Fuqua, Nancy
Gainer, Joy
Garretson, Nancy
Gibson, Joanne
Grady, Marla
Grotheer, Joshua
Hagan, Lynn
Hamm, Donna
Harlan, Glena
Harn, Sandra
Hartmann, Nancy
Hartmann, Jackie

Harvard, Mary
Haynes, Jeanne
Herrin, Laura
Herrin, Mary
Hester, Illena
Hines, Betsy
Holland, Judy
Hook, Lou
Hughes, Amy
Hughes, Nancy
Hunsberger, Margaret
Hylbert, Char
Jordan, Matra
Kleine, Susan
Kraft, Kim
Lemack, Karen
Lindsey, Libby
Mallory, Ann
Mallory, John
Martin, Linda
Martin, Melody
Massey, Nina
Mayo, Jeanette
McCarthy, Lisa Coker
McCook, Linda
McDonald, Karen
McNeilly, Beth
Meyer, Chic
Meyer, Linda
Montford, Nancy
Morris, Johnnie
Murphy, Gail
Nash, Debbie
Nesbit, Martha
Nettles, Sarah
Newton, Eva
Norris, Bobbie
Oliver, Vicki
Pease, Don
Phillips, Cindy
Phillips, Dianna
Quattlebaum, Fall
Quattlebaum, Robin &
   Michelle
Quattlebaum, Ruth
Rainey, Jane
Ramage, Patty
Ramstad, Sandy

Reese, June
Richards, Betty
Richey, Bunnie
Rippey, Sonya
Rogers, Deborah B.
Ronning, Patty
Rush, Barbara
Scarbrough, Lea
Schwandt, Willi
Schloenbach, Bobbie
Scott, Carole
Scott, Sally
Sherrill, Ann
Shuman, Diane
Sills, Nancy
Simmons, Jeannie
Sloan, Martha
Smiley, Nancy
Smith, Louise
Smith, Melinda
South, Donna
Sowell, Barbara
Starr, Linda
Tanner, Kathryn
Thomas, Richard
Thomas, Shannon
Troughton, Lynn
Tully, Donna
Usher, Elizabeth
Vach, Jan
Vann, Julie
Vaughan, Sallie
Vaughan, Scott
Walker, Ellen
Wallace, Laurine
Wardell, Eloise
Way, Judy
West, Kay
Williams, M'liss
Williams, Willie
Windom, Herb
Windom, Tricia
Yannett, Lisa
Yeckley, Dana
Yeckley, Jay
Young, Shirley
Zelinsky, Marjolein
Zittrouer, Faye

Super Starters
& Snacks

A Low-Country Island

Isle of Hope is one of the many low-country islands found along the coasts of Georgia and South Carolina. Many were settled by Indians before the English arrived and some retained Indian names. While the origin of Isle of Hope's name is not sure, there are a few different theories and legends.

Legend has it that before the English settled in the Savannah area, the Isle of Hope was called Oope Island by the Indians. Early colonial records from 1740 state that the island was first named Parkersburg after one of its first residents, Henry Parker. Later the name was changed to Isle of Hope by John Fallowfield, Noble Jones and Henry Parker, whose families owned huge plantations on the island. Other sources say the French called it *L'Isle d'Esperance,* which translated means Isle of Hope. Following the upheaval of revolution, the island may indeed have been a place of refuge and hope.

Tradition tells us that the island was literally an Isle of Hope for the many Savannah families who fled to it, living in tents during the yellow fever epidemic in 1820. This dreaded disease claimed the lives of many Savannahians.

Regardless of how the island really came to be called Isle of Hope, most of its residents would agree that it is fittingly named.

Dips and Spreads

Southwestern

Cheese Appetizers

Seafood and Meat Appetizers

Vegetable Appetizers

Mustards

Baked Cheese

1 round loaf bread	1 (4-ounce) can chopped green chilies
1 (8-ounce) container sour cream	
1 (6-ounce) jar dried chipped beef	2 cups grated sharp Cheddar cheese
1 (8-ounce) package cream cheese, softened	

Preheat oven to 300°. Hollow out bread leaving 1½ inch edges. Mix remaining ingredients and place in bread. Wrap well with aluminum foil and bake for 1½ hours. Serve with large Fritos or Scoops.

Variation
Vegetarian Baked Cheese

2 cups chopped spinach can be substituted for chopped beef for vegetarians.

Confetti Dip

1 cup cottage cheese	2 tablespoons chives, chopped
1 tablespoon lemon juice	2 tablespoons pimento, chopped
⅓ cup mayonnaise	½ teaspoon garlic powder
2 tablespoons chopped onion	

Combine cottage cheese and lemon juice in electric blender and blend until smooth. Mix together with other ingredients. Chill. Serve as dip with vegetable tray.

Yield: 1½ cups

Corn Dip

4 ounces butter or margarine	1 (8-ounce) can corn, drained
1 (8-ounce) package cream cheese, softened	2-3 jalapeños, chopped

Preheat oven to 300°. Mix all ingredients and bake for 15 minutes. Serve with Fritos or corn chips.

Yield: 1½ to 2 cups

Double Dill Dip

1 cup coarsely chopped refrigerated kosher dill pickles

1 (8-ounce) package cream cheese, softened

¼ cup sour cream

1 tablespoon chopped fresh dill weed

Dill sprigs for garnish

1 clove garlic, minced, optional

3 dashes Tabasco sauce, optional

Place pickles in food processor and process until finely chopped. Add remaining ingredients and process until well blended. Cover and chill 2 hours. Garnish with dill weed. Serve with tortilla chips or with vegetable tray.

Yield: 2 cups

Mediterranean Artichoke Dip

1 lemon

4 anchovy fillets, drained and dried with paper towel

1 (14-ounce) can artichoke hearts, drained

½ cup loosely packed fresh parsley

½ cup grated Parmesan cheese

½ cup mayonnaise

¼ cup olive oil

Grate 1 teaspoon zest from lemon and then squeeze. Blend lemon zest and juice with remaining ingredients in food processor until smooth. Scrape into bowl and chill. Serve on toast rounds or sesame crisps. Will keep in refrigerator up to 1 week.

Historical Note: Artichokes are one of the oldest foods known to humans. In the 16th century, this delicacy was reserved for men only. The artichoke is a perennial in the thistle family and the "vegetable" we eat is actually the plant's flower bud.

Shrimp Spread Delight

1 pound raw shrimp

1 (8-ounce) package cream cheese, softened

½ cup finely chopped green onions

3 tablespoons lemon juice

2 tablespoons chopped fresh parsley

½ teaspoons salt

⅛ teaspoon cayenne pepper

½ cup mayonnaise

Boil, peel, devein and chop shrimp. In bowl blend cream cheese with remaining ingredients. Fold in shrimp. Cover and refrigerate. Serve with crackers or fresh celery and carrot sticks.

Smoked Oyster Dip

1 (8-ounce) package cream
   cheese, softened
1 (6-ounce) can black olives,
   chopped

1 (3¾-ounce) can smoked
   oysters, drained and chopped
⅓ cup mayonnaise
1 tablespoon lemon juice
   Salt to taste

Mix all ingredients together and refrigerate. Serve with crackers.

Yield: 2 cups

Swiss and Bacon Dip

1 (8-ounce) package cream
   cheese
½ cup mayonnaise
1 cup grated Swiss cheese

2-3 tablespoons sliced green onions
1 sleeve Ritz crackers, crushed
8 slices cooked bacon, crumbled

Preheat oven to 400°. Mix first 4 ingredients. Top with Ritz crackers and then top with bacon. Bake for 20 minutes. Serve with Ritz crackers or Triscuits.

Yield: 2 cups

Tomato Chutney

1 (14-ounce) can chopped
   tomatoes, undrained
1 medium onion, finely chopped
2 bell peppers, finely chopped
1 cup light brown sugar

½ cup granulated sugar
2 tablespoons ketchup
1 teaspoon black pepper
   Jalapeño pepper to taste

Mix all ingredients in saucepan. Bring to boil, simmer covered for 2 hours. Cook down without lid for thicker consistency. Serve over block of cream cheese or as sauce with meat.

Yield: 2 to 3 cups

Black-Eyed Pea Salsa

1 (16-ounce) can black-eyed peas, drained
1 (15-ounce) can shoe peg corn, drained
1 jar "Braswell" pepper relish
1 can Rotel diced tomatoes and chilies, original
1 can Rotel diced tomatoes, mild
½ cup diced green pepper
½ cup diced red onion

Combine first 5 ingredients. Add green pepper and onion. Refrigerate 12 hours before serving. Serve with Fritos corn chips.

Yield: 6 cups

Red and Yellow Tomato Salsa

5 medium red tomatoes
5 yellow tomatoes
1 cup diced onion
½ cup sliced green onion
1 tablespoon minced garlic
½ cup chopped fresh basil
⅓ cup red wine vinegar
½ cup olive oil
1 teaspoon salt
½ teaspoon black pepper

Remove seeds and dice tomatoes. Add onion, garlic, basil, vinegar, oil, salt and pepper. Gently toss. Refrigerate, keeps 2 days. Serve with Tostitos chips, or serve over mild white fish.

Yield: 3 to 4 cups

Western Wraps

4 ounces cream cheese, softened
1 tablespoon taco sauce
4 (6-inch) flour tortillas
1 cup canned black beans, rinsed and drained
¼ cup real bacon pieces
½ small green pepper, diced
¼ cup (1 ounce) shredded Cheddar cheese

Stir together cream cheese and taco sauce. Spread mixture evenly on one side of each tortilla. Top with black beans and remaining ingredients. Roll tortillas tightly. Wrap in plastic wrap and chill. Cut in slices to serve.

Santa Fe Cheesecake

1½ cups finely crushed blue tortilla chips

¼ cup butter or margarine, softened

2 (8-ounce) packages cream cheese, softened

2 cups (8 ounces) shredded Monterey Jack cheese

¼ teaspoon salt

3 (8-ounce) containers sour cream, divided

3 large eggs

1 cup thick and chunky salsa

1 (4-ounce) can chopped green chilies, drained

1 (1¼-ounce) envelope taco seasoning mix

1 cup guacamole

1 medium tomato, seeded and diced

Preheat oven to 350°. Combine crushed tortilla chips and butter, and press into bottom of lightly greased 9 inch springform pan. Bake for 12 minutes and cool. Beat cream cheese, shredded cheese and salt until fluffy. Add 1 cup sour cream and beat until blended. Add eggs 1 at a time. Stir in salsa, chilies and taco seasoning. Pour into prepared crust and bake for 40 minutes or until center is almost set. Gently run knife around edge of pan to loosen. Remove sides and let cheesecake cool completely. Spread 2 cups sour cream on top. Cover and chill at least 3 hours or up to 1 day. Spread guacamole evenly on top and sprinkle with diced tomatoes. Serve with tortilla chips.

Yield: 1 (9 inch) cheesecake or 24 to 30 servings

TOMATO SANDWICHES

Few guests will pass up a tiny tomato sandwich when they're passed around at a party. Rounds are cut from soft, white bread, spread with a mayonnaise combination and topped with a slice of fresh, ripe tomato. As the Lay's commercial says, "Betcha can't eat just one."

Better Than Boursin

2 (8-ounce) packages cream
  cheese, softened
¼ cup mayonnaise
2 teaspoons Dijon mustard

2 tablespoons finely chopped
  fresh chives
2 tablespoons finely chopped
  fresh dill
1 clove garlic, minced

Beat all ingredients with electric mixer until blended. Spoon into 2 cup foil lined bowl. Cover, refrigerate overnight. Invert onto small serving plate, peel off foil and serve with crackers.

Yield: 2 cups

Bite Size Crustless Quiches

1 tablespoon butter or margarine
½ cup finely chopped red bell
  pepper
¼ cup chopped green onion
  (white and green parts)

3 large eggs
2 tablespoons milk
½ cup grated Cheddar cheese
¼ teaspoon salt
⅛ teaspoon ground black pepper

Preheat oven to 425°. Grease 24 mini muffin pan. In small saucepan, melt butter over medium heat. Add bell pepper and onion. Sauté until soft, about 5 minutes. Remove pan from heat and let mixture cool slightly. In medium sized bowl, combine eggs, milk, cheese, salt and pepper. Stir in bell pepper and onion. Fill muffin tins and bake until centers are set, 8 to 10 minutes. Cool for 1 minute. Using knife, loosen quiches around edges and remove from cups.

Yield: 24 mini quiches

Blue Cheese Puffs

1 (8-ounce) can refrigerator biscuits	¼ cup butter or margarine
	4 ounces crumbled blue cheese

Preheat oven to 400°. Cut biscuits into quarters. Arrange in two 8 inch round cake pans lined with foil for fast clean up. Melt butter and cheese together and pour over biscuit pieces, being sure to coat them all. Bake for 15 minutes or until golden brown. Serve hot.

Yield: 40 puffs

Variations
Onion Puffs

Mix 1 envelope Lipton soup mix with ¼ pound butter. Use in place of butter and blue cheese.

Parmesan Deviled Puffs

Substitute 1 (4.5-ounce) can deviled ham for blue cheese. Sprinkle tops with ¼ cup Parmesan cheese.

Crescent Wrapped Brie

1 (8-ounce) can crescent rolls	1 (10-ounce) jar raspberry or apricot preserves
1 small round Brie cheese	
1 egg, beaten	Chopped nuts, optional

Heat oven to 350°. On ungreased cookie sheet, unroll can of dough. Using half of squares, connect all perforations to form square larger than Brie round. Place Brie on center of dough. Spoon preserves over cheese. Sprinkle with nuts if desired. Use remaining crescent rolls to cover cheese (and close to form seal around cheese). Fold bottom edges up to meet top edges of dough. Top with dough cut outs to decorate. Brush with beaten egg. Bake for 20 to 25 minutes or until golden brown. Cool 10 to 15 minutes before serving.

Yield: 12 servings

Blue Cheese Crisps

¼ cup butter or margarine,
softened
1 (4-ounce) package blue cheese,
softened

¼ cup chopped pecans or walnuts
1 French baguette, cut in
(¼-inch) slices

Preheat oven to 350°. Mix butter and blue cheese. Fold in nuts. Place bread slices on cookie sheet in oven for 5 minutes. Flip over and place dollop of cheese mixture on each. Put back in oven for 3 minutes. Serve hot.

Yield: 24 slices

Cheese Onion Appetizer

1 cup mayonnaise
1 cup chopped onion

1 cup shredded Cheddar, Swiss,
Parmesan or mozzarella
cheese

Preheat oven to 375°. Mix all ingredients and spoon into baking dish. Bake for 20 to 30 minutes or until cheese is melted and bubbly. Serve with raw vegetables or crackers. Spice it up with few dashes of pepper sauce.

Cheese Onion Ring

2 (12-ounce) packages shredded
sharp Cheddar cheese
1 cup chopped onion
1 cup chopped pecans

Mayonnaise
1 (10-ounce) jar raspberry or
strawberry jam

Mix cheese, onion and pecans; add enough mayonnaise to hold ingredients together to form ball. Press indentation into center of ball. Chill. When ready to serve fill indentation with raspberry jam and serve with crackers.

Cheesy Curry Appetizer Wedges

1 cup olives, chopped	⅓ cup mayonnaise
½ cup chopped green onions	½ teaspoon curry powder
1½ cups grated sharp Cheddar	¼ teaspoon salt
cheese	6 English muffins

Preheat oven to 400°. Mix all spread ingredients together. Spread on split muffins. Place on baking sheet, cut into fourths. Bake for 10 minutes. Best served warm.

Yield: 48 wedges

Fillet of Beef and Arugula Crostini

HORSERADISH SPREAD

¼ cup mayonnaise	2 finely chopped green onions
¼ cup sour cream	2 teaspoons prepared
1 teaspoon Dijon mustard	horseradish

ASSEMBLY

2 cups coarsely chopped arugula (discard coarse stems)	36 pieces cooked filet mignon or flank steak sliced thin
36 (½-inch thick) baguette slices, buttered and toasted lightly	Parmesan cheese, fresh shaved

Prepare spread by combining all ingredients. Cover each baguette slice with horseradish spread. Top with arugula, piece of fillet and Parmesan curl.

Yield: 36 appetizers

Variation
Artichoke Spread

2 (6-ounce) jars marinated artichoke hearts, rinsed and drained	¼ cup white-wine vinegar
	½ cup olive oil
1 clove garlic	

Purée all ingredients. Use in place of horseradish spread.

Krispy Cheese Wafers

1 cup (2 sticks) butter or margarine

16 ounces grated sharp Cheddar cheese

2 cups all-purpose flour

½ teaspoon Tabasco sauce

3 cups corn flakes or Rice Krispies

Preheat oven to 350°. Mix all ingredients in food processor. Form into small balls and flatten with fork. Bake for 15 to 20 minutes.

Bacon Roll Ups

1 (3-ounce) package cream cheese, softened

3-4 green onions, chopped

½ teaspoon garlic salt or powder

Salt and pepper to taste

Milk

ASSEMBLY

Loaf of white bread

1 pound package bacon

Preheat oven to 400°. Combine cream cheese, green onions, garlic salt and salt and pepper. Use milk to thin to spreading consistency. Cut crusts off bread and roll flat with rolling pin. Spread with cream cheese mixture. Cut each slice in thirds, roll up and wrap in third of slice of bacon. (May be refrigerated or frozen at this point.) Bake for 8 to 10 minutes, flip rolls over with spatula, and bake for another 5 to 8 minutes. Drain on paper towels and serve warm.

Yield: 16 appetizers

BRIE WITH KAHLÚA AND PECANS

Mix 3 tablespoons packed brown sugar and ¼ cup Kahlúa (or strong freshly brewed coffee, cooled). Heat in skillet, stirring constantly until blended. Add ¾ cup toasted pecans and cook until hot. Remove from heat. Microwave round of Brie for 1 to 2 minutes to soften and pour warm mixture over cheese.

Greek Chicken Fingers with Plum Sauce

12	boneless chicken breasts	1	teaspoon salt
1½	cups buttermilk	1	teaspoon black pepper
2	tablespoons lemon juice	2	cloves garlic, minced
2	teaspoons Worcestershire sauce	4	cups soft bread crumbs
		½	cup sesame seeds
1	teaspoon soy sauce	¼	cup butter or margarine, melted
1	teaspoon paprika		
1	tablespoon Greek seasonings	¼	cup shortening, melted

Cut chicken in ½ inch strips. Combine next 9 ingredients and mix with chicken until well-coated. Cover and refrigerate overnight. Preheat oven to 350°. Drain chicken thoroughly. Combine bread crumbs and sesame seeds, mixing well. Add chicken and toss to coat. Place chicken in two greased 9 x 13 inch baking dishes. Mix butter and shortening; brush on chicken. Bake for 35 to 40 minutes. Serve with Plum Sauce.

PLUM SAUCE

1½	cups red plum jam	1½	tablespoons horseradish
1½	tablespoons mustard	1½	teaspoons lemon juice

Combine all ingredients in small saucepan, mixing well. Place over low heat just until warm, stirring constantly.

Yield: 12 to 14 appetizer servings

Crab Appetizer

1	pound fresh crabmeat	2	tablespoons mayonnaise
1	(7-ounce) jar Old English cheese	½	tablespoon seasoning salt
			Dash of Worcestershire sauce
½	cup butter or margarine, softened	1	package English muffins, split and quartered

Mix all spread ingredients together. Spread on muffin quarters. Place on cookie sheet and freeze at least 1 hour. Can be bagged and stored in freezer for future use. Take out amount needed and broil from frozen until hot and bubbly; approximately 8 to 10 minutes.

Yield: 48 pieces

Baked Crab Appetizer Casserole

2 (8-ounce) packages cream cheese, softened	1 teaspoon dry mustard
1 (8-ounce) carton sour cream	¼ teaspoon garlic salt
¼ cup mayonnaise	¼ teaspoon salt (or more to taste)
2 tablespoons Worcestershire sauce	1 cup grated Cheddar cheese, divided
2 tablespoons lemon juice	1 pound fresh lump crabmeat, gently squeezed to drain

Preheat oven to 350°. Combine first 8 ingredients; stir until blended. Fold in half grated cheese. Fold in crabmeat. Spoon mixture into 7 x 11 or 8 x 8 inch baking dish. Sprinkle evenly with remaining cheese. Bake for 35 minutes or until bubbly. Can be served hot or at room temperature. Serve with crackers. May be assembled day before and refrigerated until ready to bake.

Yield: 12 appetizer servings

Tangy Ham Meatballs

1 pound ham, ground	¾ cup cracker crumbs
¾ pound lean pork or meat loaf mix, ground	¾ cup brown sugar
½ teaspoon salt	1 teaspoon prepared mustard
⅛ teaspoon black pepper	¼ cup vinegar
1 egg, well beaten	¼ cup water
½ cup milk	Pineapple chunks

Preheat oven to 350°. Thoroughly mix first 7 ingredients and shape into small balls. Place in baking pan. Prepare glaze with next 4 ingredients and pour over ham balls. Bake uncovered for 1 hour, basting several times. Set aside to cool. Add pineapple chunks to sauce and serve piping hot. Can be frozen in sauce.

Yield: Makes 50 balls

Sausage Baguettes

1 pound hot sausage
½ cup mayonnaise
½ cup grated Cheddar cheese
½ cup grated Monterey Jack cheese

3 green onions including leaves, chopped
Garlic powder, oregano and crushed red pepper flakes to taste
2 short French bread baguettes

Preheat oven to 400°. Brown sausage until crumbly and drain fat. Mix together with remaining ingredients. Slice bread loaves in half horizontally and spread with sausage mixture. Place on cookie sheet and bake for 10 to 15 minutes until lightly browned and bubbly. Cut into small slices and serve. Makes the house smell great as it cooks and big hit with the men!

Yield: 10 to 12 appetizer servings

Sausage Cheese Pinwheels

1 (16-ounce) package bulk sausage
1 (8-ounce) package cream cheese

2 (8-ounce) cans crescent rolls
Dash Worcestershire sauce, optional

Brown sausage in large frying pan and drain fat. Mix cream cheese into sausage over low heat until melted and thoroughly blended. Cool slightly. Separate crescent rolls into rectangles on cookie sheet. Spread sausage mixture evenly over rolls. Starting at the long side, roll up. Freeze until hard enough to slice. After slicing, can be frozen until needed. Either defrost or cook frozen, adding 2 to 3 minutes to cooking time. Preheat oven to 375°. Bake for 11 to 13 minutes.

Yield: 36 to 40 slices, depending on thickness of slices

MINI CRAB CAKES

Using any crab cake recipe, make mini cakes. Sauté in butter and serve on toast rounds with dollop of tarter sauce.

Shrimp 'N Grits Tarts

3¾ cups chicken broth, divided
1 cup milk
¼ cup butter or margarine, divided
½ teaspoon white pepper
1 cup uncooked grits
⅔ cup shredded Parmesan cheese
⅔ cup chopped ham
3 tablespoons all-purpose flour

3 tablespoons chopped fresh parsley
1 teaspoon Worcestershire for Chicken (Zesty Herb and Spice Marinade)
36 small shrimp, cooked, peeled and deveined
Chopped parsley to garnish

Preheat oven to 350°. Bring 2 cups chicken broth, milk, 2 tablespoons butter and white pepper to boil over medium high heat. Gradually whisk in grits, return to boil. Reduce heat and simmer, stirring occasionally, 5 to 10 minutes or until thickened. Add cheese and whisk until melted and blended. Spoon 1 small teaspoon of grits mixture into 36 lightly greased mini muffin tins. Bake for 20 to 25 minutes or until lightly browned. Make deep indentation in center of warm grits tarts. Let cool in pans. Remove tarts from muffin tins and place on jelly roll pan. Melt remaining 2 tablespoons butter over medium high heat, add ham and sauté 1 to 2 minutes. Sprinkle 3 tablespoons flour evenly over ham and cook, stirring often, 1 to 2 minutes or until lightly browned. Gradually add remaining 1¼ cups chicken broth, stirring until smooth. Reduce heat and cook, stirring often, 5 to 10 minutes or until thickened. Stir in 3 tablespoons parsley and Worcestershire and spoon evenly into tarts. Top each with 1 shrimp. Bake 5 to 10 minutes or until just warm. Garnish.

Yield: 36 tarts

Shrimp or Crab Newberg

2 tablespoons butter or margarine
2 tablespoons all-purpose flour
2 cups half-and-half, divided

1 can cream of celery soup
1 pound coarsely chopped shrimp or 1 pound crabmeat
½ cup sherry

Make thick white sauce as follows: Melt margarine and remove from heat. Mix in flour until smooth. Add 1 cup half-and-half, stirring well so that sauce remains smooth. Add remaining cup half-and-half and return to burner to thicken. Stir in soup and seafood. Slowly stir in sherry. Serve hot in chaffing dish with pastry shells.

Shrimp Vinaigrette Wrapped In Snow Peas

1 bay leaf	1 pound large shrimp, peeled and deveined

VINAIGRETTE

½ cup olive oil	1 clove garlic, minced
3 tablespoons white wine vinegar	1 tablespoon chopped fresh dill
1 tablespoon chopped shallots	Pinch of sugar
1 teaspoon finely minced fresh ginger	Salt and pepper to taste

ASSEMBLY
15-20 snow peas

Add bay leaf to large pot of water and bring to boil. Add shrimp and cook, stirring constantly, until just done (2 to 3 minutes). Be sure not to overcook. Drain shrimp, immerse in very cold water to cool and drain again. Mix vinaigrette ingredients in covered jar. Shake well and pour over shrimp. Cover and refrigerate 1 to 2 days, tossing every 12 hours. String peas and blanch in boiling water for 30 seconds. Drain and immerse in iced water. Drain again. Split pods lengthwise so you have 30 to 40 separate halves. Wrap pea pod around each shrimp and fasten with round natural wood toothpick. Serve cold or room temperature.

Yield: 30 to 40 shrimp

Note: In place of snow pea, wrap each shrimp with paper thin piece of prosciutto.

Pin Wheel Shrimp

4½ cups cooked shrimp, peeled, deveined and chopped	2 teaspoons chili sauce
¼ cup mayonnaise	1 tablespoon chopped celery
2 tablespoons green olives	1 (8-ounce) can crescent rolls

Combine first 5 ingredients. Separate crescent rolls into rectangles. Spread mixture onto dough and roll up starting with long side. Refrigerate several hours. When ready to bake, preheat oven to 375°, slice into ¼ inch slices and bake for 10 to 15 minutes.

Smoked Salmon with Norwegian Sauce

Fresh salmon steaks
Soy sauce

Dark brown sugar

NORWEGIAN SAUCE

⅓ cup mayonnaise

⅓ cup mustard

⅓ cup horseradish

Marinate salmon in soy sauce overnight. Apply generous amount of brown sugar to one side of salmon. Smoke in electric smoker for 2 to 2 ½ hours. Wood chips that have been soaked in water overnight can be placed on stones around the heating element. Mix sauce ingredients. Serve as an appetizer on crackers with Norwegian sauce

Variation
Smoked Fish

2 quarts water

1 cup non-iodized salt

½ cup brown sugar

¼ cup fresh lemon juice

4 tablespoons garlic powder

1 teaspoon onion powder

Combine all ingredients and marinate fish for at least 4 hours. When ready to smoke, rinse and dry fish. Smoke until cooked.

Asparagus Roll-Ups

1 (8-ounce) package cream cheese, softened

4 ounces blue cheese, softened

1 egg, well beaten

1 (15-ounce) can asparagus spears, drained

1 large loaf sandwich bread

1 cup (2 sticks) butter or margarine, melted

Preheat oven to 400°. Mix cream cheese and blue cheese and add egg. Trim crusts from bread and roll thin with rolling pin. Spread each slice with cheese. Lay asparagus spear across bread, using more than 1 if thin. Roll up and cut each slice into thirds. Dip each into melted butter and place on baking sheet. Bake for 15 to 20 minutes. Serve warm.

Yield: About 6 dozen pieces

Bruschetta

4 ripe tomatoes
1 clove garlic, chopped or
minced
2 tablespoons olive oil
2 tablespoons chopped fresh
basil
¼ cup chopped shallots or green
onions

Splash of vinegar
Salt and pepper
1 loaf French or Italian bread,
sliced
¼ cup goat cheese
¼ cup olive oil

Preheat oven to 375°. Cut tomatoes in quarters; gently squeeze seeds out and dice. Add next 6 ingredients and mix. Lay bread on baking sheet. Brush lightly with olive oil and bake for 10 minutes or until golden and crisp. Spread goat cheese on toasted bread and spoon tomato mixture on top.

Gorgonzola and Caramelized Onions

2 tablespoons butter or
margarine
2 medium onions, sliced and
separated into rings
1 tablespoon packed brown
sugar

1 teaspoon balsamic vinegar
8 (½-inch thick) slices baguette
2 tablespoons crumbled
Gorgonzola cheese

Melt margarine in 10 inch skillet over medium heat. Add onions, brown sugar and vinegar and cook about 25 minutes, stirring frequently, until onions are golden brown. Set oven control to broil. Place baguette slices on ungreased cookie sheet. Broil with tops 2 to 3 inches from heat 1 to 2 minutes or until lightly toasted. Remove from oven and spoon caramelized onions evenly onto each baguette slice. Sprinkle with cheese. Broil about 1 minute or until cheese is melted.

Yield: 8 servings

ROASTED PARTY PECANS

Toss 1 cup unsalted pecan halves in 1 tablespoon butter mixed with 1 tablespoon Worcestershire sauce. Roast in shallow pan in 275° oven for 30 minutes, stirring often. Drain on paper towel; sprinkle with salt.

Pesto Sun-Dried Tomato Torte

2   (8-ounce) packages cream
    cheese, softened
½   cup grated Parmesan cheese
2   cloves garlic, finely chopped

3-6 ounces julienne cut sun-dried
    tomatoes
4   ounces basil pesto

Mix cream cheese, Parmesan cheese and garlic until blended. Divide in half. Line 3 cup mold (or bowl) with plastic wrap, overlapping 3 inches. Coat plastic wrap with cooking spray. Spread sun-dried tomatoes in bottom of bowl. Carefully press half cream cheese mixture on top of tomatoes. Spread pesto over cream cheese and finish by pressing remaining half cream cheese mixture over pesto. Fold overhanging plastic wrap over top to cover. Refrigerate until firm, at least 1 hour. To serve, invert mold onto serving platter and remove plastic. Serve with thinly sliced baguette or bagel chips.

Spicy Spinach Pinwheels

2   (10-ounce) packages frozen
    chopped spinach, thawed
1   cup sour cream
1   (8-ounce) package cream
    cheese, softened
1   cup mayonnaise
1   teaspoon minced fresh jalapeño
1   teaspoon minced fresh garlic
6   green onions, chopped
½   cup chopped black olives

1   (4-ounce) can chopped green
    chilies
¼   teaspoon hot pepper sauce
1   envelope ranch salad dressing
    mix
1   (8-ounce) can chopped water
    chestnuts, drained
2   teaspoons chili powder
10 large flour tortillas

Squeeze excess moisture from spinach. Combine all ingredients except tortillas in large bowl: mix well. Spread spinach mixture on each flour tortilla; roll to enclose filling. Wrap each tortilla tightly in waxed paper. Place in zip plastic food storage bag or in airtight container. Chill overnight. Unwrap and cut tortillas into slices before serving.

Yield: 50 to 60 pieces

Shrimp Mold or Loaf

1	(10¾-ounce) can tomato soup	¾	cup finely chopped celery
1	(8-ounce) package cream cheese	¾	cup finely chopped onions
1	package unflavored gelatin	¾	cup finely chopped green pepper
¼	cup water	2	cups cooked, peeled and deveined small shrimp
1	cup mayonnaise		

In saucepan, heat soup and cream cheese; whisk until smooth. Cool. Dissolve gelatin in water and add to soup mixture. Stir in mayonnaise and then vegetables. In lightly oiled mold or loaf pan, layer soup mixture and shrimp in alternate layers, ending with soup. Refrigerate overnight. Serve with crackers.

Mighty Hot Mustard

1	(4-ounce) can dry mustard	1	cup sugar
1	cup cider vinegar		Pinch of salt
2	eggs	1½	cups mayonnaise

Mix dry mustard and vinegar and let stand overnight in refrigerator. The next day, add eggs, sugar and salt, and cook in double boiler until thick. Let cool and beat in mayonnaise. On the hot side. Keeps indefinitely in refrigerator or can be jarred or frozen.

Yield: 1 pint

Tewkesbury Mustard

2	cups dry mustard	¼	cup parsley flakes
2	cups all-purpose flour	2	teaspoons dried marjoram
¼	cup salt	2	teaspoons dried rosemary
2	cups sugar	2	teaspoons dried thyme
3	cloves garlic, finely crushed	2	teaspoons dried sage
2	tablespoons dried basil	3-4	cups white vinegar

Mix dry ingredients and garlic. Add vinegar. Stir constantly, using wire whisk, until mixture is smooth and free of lumps. Let mixture stand overnight. Stir again next morning and add more vinegar if mixture seems too thick. Store in refrigerator.

Yield: 15 to 18 (4-ounce) jars

Note: Great as Christmas gifts or hostesses thank yous.

Breakfast, Brunch & Breads

Moss and Marshes

Two distinct characteristics of low country islands like Isle of Hope are the Spanish Moss seen hanging in streamers from the trees and the tidal salt marshes. The name Spanish Moss is misleading because these plants are not found in Spain and are not mosses. Native Americans called the plant Tree Hair, which the French explorers changed to Barbe Espagnole (Spanish Beard) to insult their bitter rivals in the New World. Spanish Moss, a milder variation of the French taunt, has survived. Another common name is Gray Beard.

This plant grows only where the climate is warm and the air is very humid. It is not a parasite but will grow only on trees, and can absorb water up to ten times its dry weight. Thus, it is very useful as mulch for potted plants, but can actually crack the branch on which it grows after a heavy rainfall. Over the years, it has been used as insulation and stuffing for items such as dolls, pillows and mattresses. Because it also harbors small insects and spiders, there is a legend that this stuffing may give rise to the nursery rhyme, *Night, Night, Sleep Tight, Don't Let the Bed Bugs Bite.*

Like Spanish Moss, salt marshes are plentiful in the Isle of Hope area. The most common of the salt marsh plants in Georgia is a tall, cane-like grass called Smooth Cord Grass (Spartina) which virtually covers the coastal marsh area. These plants are hardy with extensive underground structures that hold the marsh together and slow erosion. The salt marsh is responsible for the continuation and survival of the balance of nature within the estuarine ecology. The tide is truly the life blood of the marsh, nourishing the grasses and transporting food and nutrients produced by the marsh to the sea. The marshes support an abundance of fish, shellfish, birds and wildlife, and act as giant filters to cleanse the water of the low country. They serve as a primary nursery ground for young fish, crabs, shrimp, etc which in turn sustain larger fish and the cycle goes on and on.

Additionally, our salt marshes act as buffers against offshore storms. Without their dissipating effect, hurricanes and Northeasters would do much more damage.

Brunch Casseroles and Stratas

Quiches and Soufflés

Fruit Sides

Miscellaneous

Breads

Muffins and Biscuits

Baked Eggs Provençal

1	tablespoon olive oil	½	teaspoon dried tarragon or basil
1	tablespoon butter or margarine		
6	eggs	¼	teaspoon salt
2	ounces Gruyère cheese, coarsely grated (½ cup)	¼	teaspoon ground black pepper
		2	medium-size tomatoes, sliced
2	green onions, chopped		

Preheat oven to 400°. In shallow 8 inch square baking dish, place oil and butter. Place dish in oven to melt butter. In large bowl, beat eggs lightly; stir in grated cheese, chopped onion, tarragon, salt and pepper. Remove dish from oven; swirl to coat it evenly with oil mixture. Pour egg mixture and arrange tomato slices on top. Bake until eggs are just set, about 15 minutes, and serve.

Yield: 4 to 6 servings

Baked French Toast

½	cup butter	5	eggs
¾	cup light brown sugar	1	tablespoon frozen orange juice concentrate
1	teaspoon cinnamon		
1	loaf soft French bread (cut in 1 to 1½-inch slices)	1½	cups half-and-half

Melt butter in 9 x 13 inch baking dish. Combine sugar and cinnamon. Sprinkle third sugar mixture into butter and gently stir. Arrange bread on top of sugar mixture in baking dish. Keep snug, but not squeezed. Sprinkle remaining sugar mixture over bread. Beat eggs with half-and-half and orange juice. Pour evenly over bread. Cover and refrigerate overnight. Preheat oven to 300° and bake for 35 to 45 minutes. Serve warm with hot syrup.

Yield: 8 to 10 servings

Note: For healthier version, substitute whole grain bread for French bread, reduce butter to ¼ cup and use milk or non fat half-and-half.

Company Brunch Eggs

18 eggs
¼ cup cream or milk
½ teaspoon salt
¼ cup (½ stick) butter or
    margarine
1½ cups sour cream

1 pound bacon or ham cooked
    and diced
1 (8-ounce) can mushrooms,
    drained
2 cups grated Cheddar cheese

Butter 9 x 13 inch casserole dish and set aside. In large frying pan melt butter. Beat eggs with cream and salt. Cook eggs in frying pan; do not over cook (they should be quite runny). Put in prepared casserole and spread sour cream over eggs. Sprinkle with bacon or ham, mushrooms and cheese. Cover casserole and refrigerate overnight. Preheat oven to 350°. Bake for 30 minutes or until heated through.

Yield: 12 servings

Hash Brown and Sausage Brunch Casserole

1 pound bulk sausage
1 medium onion, chopped
2 pounds frozen hash brown
    potatoes, thawed
    (cube style)
8 eggs, beaten
12 ounces evaporated milk
½ cup milk

½ teaspoon salt
½ teaspoon dried basil
½ teaspoon dried oregano
½ teaspoon leaf thyme
½ teaspoon garlic powder
⅛ teaspoon black pepper
1-1½ cups shredded cheese
    (Cheddar or Jack)

Preheat oven 350°. Grease 9 x 13 inch baking dish. Brown sausage and onion; drain. Set aside. Spread potatoes evenly in prepared dish. Add sausage and onion on top of potatoes. Mix eggs, evaporated milk, milk and all spices. Pour mixture over potatoes and sausage in baking dish. Sprinkle cheese on top. Bake for 60 to 65 minutes or until set.

Yield: 8 to 10 servings

Raisin Bread and Maple Syrup Strata

8-12	slices cinnamon raisin bread		Cinnamon
½	cup maple syrup	6	eggs
½	cup raisins, separated	1½	cups milk
½	cup chopped pecans	½	teaspoon vanilla
1	(8-ounce) package cream cheese, cut into cubes		

Grease 9 x 13 inch baking dish. Place layer of raisin bread in bottom of baking dish. Pour syrup over bread layer. Sprinkle with ¼ cup of raisins, pecans and half of cream cheese cubes. Sprinkle lightly with cinnamon. Add another layer of raisin bread. Beat together eggs, milk, and vanilla; pour over bread. Sprinkle with remaining raisins and cream cheese cubes. Sprinkle lightly with cinnamon again. Refrigerate overnight. Preheat oven to 350° and bake for 45 to 50 minutes or until bubbly. Serve warm with extra syrup.

Yield: 8 to 10 servings

Sausage or Ham Egg Strata

8	slices white bread, trimmed and buttered	16	eggs
1	pound pork or turkey sausage cooked and crumbled or ham diced	1½	cups milk
		1	teaspoon salt
		1	teaspoon Worcestershire sauce
1-1½	cups shredded sharp Cheddar cheese		Dash of Tabasco sauce

Line 9 x 13 inch buttered baking dish with buttered white bread. Cover with cooked, drained meat. Add cheese. Beat eggs and milk with spices and pour over cheese. Cover and refrigerate overnight. Preheat oven to 300°. Bake uncovered for 1 hour.

Yield: 15 servings

Variation
Vegetable Egg Strata

½ red pepper, cut up and 1 head broccoli, cut up and steamed or 1 pound asparagus cut up and steamed can be substituted for meat.

Sky-High Brunch Bake

1 (17⅓-ounce) package frozen puff pastry (2 sheets), thawed
6 eggs
1 cup ricotta cheese
   Dash of Tabasco sauce

2 (10-ounce) packages chopped frozen spinach, thawed and well drained
4 slices cooked bacon, chopped
1½ cups grated Cheddar cheese
1 cup chopped red pepper

Preheat oven to 400°. Unfold puff pastry sheets; roll 1 sheet to 11 inch square and other 12 inch square. Line bottom and side of greased springform pan with 12 inch pastry square. Beat eggs, reserving 1 tablespoon. Add ricotta, Tabasco and spinach to eggs; blending well. Layer half each of bacon, Cheddar cheese, spinach mixture and peppers in pastry-lined pan. Repeat layers. Place other pastry square over mixture; fold and tuck pastry edges into pan to enclose filling. Pinch edges to seal. Brush surface with reserved egg; pierce pastry several times to form vents for steam to escape during baking. Bake for 45 to 55 minutes or until top is golden brown. Cool 10 minutes then run knife around edge of pan before removing.

Yield: 12 servings

Southwestern Brunch Strata

1 pound mild ground sausage
1 small onion, chopped
½ green pepper, chopped
2 (10-ounce) cans diced tomatoes and green chilies
6 (10-inch) flour tortillas, torn into bite-size pieces

3 cups (12 ounces) shredded Jack cheese blend
6 eggs
2 cups milk
1 teaspoon salt
½ teaspoon ground black pepper

Sauté sausage until no longer pink and crumbled. Drain and return to pan; add onion and green pepper and sauté for 5 minutes or until vegetables are tender. Stir in tomatoes and chilies, and simmer for 10 minutes. Layer half each tortilla pieces, sausage mixture and cheese in 9 x 13 inch greased baking dish. Repeat layers. Whisk eggs, milk, salt and pepper together; pour over. Cover and refrigerate for 8 hours. Preheat oven to 350°. Bake for 50 to 60 minutes or until bubbly and golden.

Yield: 10 to 12 servings

Spinach Feta Strata

1 medium onion, chopped fine	8 cups 1 inch cubes French bread
1 red pepper, cut into thin strips	
3 tablespoons butter or margarine	1½ cups coarsely grated Monterey Jack cheese
1 teaspoon salt, divided	9 large eggs, beaten
½ teaspoon black pepper, divided	2¾ cups whole milk
¼ teaspoon freshly grated nutmeg	7 ounces crumbled Feta cheese
1 (10-ounce) package chopped spinach, thawed and drained well	

Grease 3 quart baking dish. Sauté onions and pepper in butter. Add ½ teaspoon salt, ¼ teaspoon pepper and nutmeg and cook, stirring, for 1 minute. Stir in drained spinach and set aside. Spread one third of bread cubes in baking dish. Top with one third of spinach mixture. Sprinkle with one third of Jack cheese. Repeat layering 2 more times. In medium bowl, combine eggs, milk, remaining ½ teaspoon salt and ¼ teaspoon pepper and pour evenly over strata. Sprinkle Feta cheese on top. Cover and refrigerate overnight. Preheat oven to 350°. Bake uncovered for 45 to 55 minutes or until lightly browned.

Yield: 6 to 8 servings

Ham Quiche

1½ cups diced ham	2 eggs, beaten
8 ounces Swiss cheese, grated	½ cup milk
⅓ cup finely chopped green onion	1 frozen (9-inch) deep dish pie shell, unbaked
2 tablespoons all-purpose flour	
1 cup mayonnaise	

Preheat oven to 350°. Mix all ingredients together and pour into unbaked pie shell. Bake for 1 hour.

Yield: 1 (9-inch) quiche

Impossible Quiche

12 slices bacon (about ½ pound), crispy fried and crumbled
1 cup shredded Swiss cheese (about 4 ounces)
⅓ cup chopped onion
2 cups milk
1 cup biscuit baking mix
4 eggs
¼ teaspoon salt
⅛ teaspoon black pepper

Preheat oven to 400°. Lightly grease (10 inch) pie plate. Sprinkle bacon, cheese and onion in pie plate. Beat remaining ingredients until smooth; 15 seconds in blender on high speed or 1 minute with hand mixer. Pour evenly into pie plate. Bake until top is golden brown and knife inserted in center comes out clean, about 30 minutes. Let stand 5 minutes before cutting. Garnish with tomato slices and extra fried bacon strips.

Yield: 6 to 8 servings

Breakfast Pie

1 frozen (9-inch) deep dish pie shell
1 pound sausage, crumbled, fried and drained
1½ cups grated mozzarella cheese
¾ cup milk
4 eggs, beaten
½ teaspoon salt
¼ teaspoon pepper

Preheat oven to 350°. Layer sausage and cheese in frozen pie shell. Mix milk, eggs, salt and pepper; pour into pie shell. Bake for 45 minutes. Serve hot.

Yield: 1 (9-inch) pie

Variations
Luncheon Pie

Use 1 pound shrimp, ¼ cup sliced green onion, and 1½ cups Swiss cheese.

Dinner Pie

Slice 2 tomatoes into pie shell, then layer 1 pound cooked ground beef and 1½ cups Cheddar cheese.

No Fail Bacon and Cheese Soufflés

3	tablespoons butter or margarine	1	tablespoon Dijon mustard
3	tablespoons all-purpose flour		10-12 slices cooked bacon, crumbled
¾	cup milk	4	eggs, separated
¾	cup shredded sharp Cheddar cheese		

Preheat oven to 350°. Melt butter and stir in flour. Cook 1 minute. Gradually add milk, stirring until well blended. Cook and stir until mixture comes to boil. Remove from heat. Add cheese, stirring until melted. Stir in mustard and bacon. Cool slightly. Beat in egg yolks, one at a time. Beat egg whites until stiff, but not dry, about 5 minutes. Gently fold into yolk mixture. Pour into 12 lightly greased muffin tins. Bake for 25 minutes or until puffed and set.

Yield: 12 muffin-size soufflés

Cranberry Apple Crumble

3	cups peeled chopped apples	½	cup all-purpose flour
2	cups fresh cranberries	1	cup quick cooking oats
1	cup sugar	½	cup chopped pecans
½	cup (1 stick) butter or margarine, melted		Pecan halves for garnish (optional)
½	cup light brown sugar, firmly packed		Fresh cranberries for garnish (optional)

Preheat oven to 325°. Place apples in bottom buttered 2 quart casserole dish. Mix cranberries and sugar and spread in dish over apples. Mix butter, brown sugar, flour, oats and nuts and spoon on top of cranberries. Garnish with pecan halves and cranberries if desired. Bake for 45 to 55 minutes.

Yield: 8 to 10 servings

Note: For firmer casserole, 2 tablespoons flour may be tossed with apples, cranberries and sugar. Three (1⅛-ounce) packages instant cinnamon and spice flavored oatmeal may be substituted for quick cooking oats.

Apple Cheese Casserole

½ cup (1 stick) butter or
   margarine, softened
1 cup sugar
2 cups grated sharp Cheddar
   cheese

¾ cup all-purpose flour
1 (15¼-ounce) can sliced
   unsweetened apples

Preheat oven to 325°. Cream butter and sugar in mixing bowl. Add cheese; combine well with hands or spoon. Add flour; mix well, batter will be stiff. Place apples in buttered 1½ quart casserole dish. Spread or pat cheese mixture over apples, covering all. Bake for 30 minutes.

Yield: 4 to 6 servings

Note: Substitute 8 ounces of Velveeta cheese for Cheddar cheese.

Breakfast Pizza

1 (8-ounce) can crescent rolls
1 pound bulk sausage, cooked
   and drained
1-1½ cups frozen hash brown
   potatoes
1 cup grated Cheddar cheese

3 eggs, beaten
½ cup milk
   Salt and pepper to taste
½ cup grated Parmesan cheese
   (optional)

Preheat oven to 375°. Unroll crescent rolls and arrange on pizza pan or baking sheet with points to center of pan making circle. When all are arranged press seams together forming crust. Form rim around edge of crust to hold ingredients in place. Sprinkle sausage, potatoes and Cheddar cheese on crust. Mix together eggs, milk, salt and pepper. Very slowly, pour egg mixture over crust. Bake for 25 to 30 minutes or until crust puffs and browns around edges. Rotate last few minutes for better browning. Sprinkle with Parmesan cheese if desired. Cut in wedges to serve.

Yield: 1 pizza

Note: Sausage can be prepared and refrigerated overnight to save time in morning.

Crabbies

1	pound mild sausage	1	tablespoon butter or margarine
2	(4-ounce) jars Old English cheese	1	package of English muffins or party rye bread

Brown sausage, drain and rinse under water. Melt cheese with butter and add to sausage. Spread on English muffins and broil for 5 to 7 minutes.

Yield: 12 muffin halves

Notes: Great for breakfast or cut into fourths and serve as an appetizer. Can be frozen. Thaw before broiling or bake frozen at 350° until bubbly.

Variation
Crabbies

Substitute 1 cup crabmeat for sausage. Combine cheese, butter, 1½ teaspoons mayonnaise and ½ teaspoon garlic salt. Add crabmeat and proceed as above.

Granola Cereal

3	cups rolled oats	¼	cup plus 2 tablespoons maple syrup
2	cups nuts (slivered almonds, or chopped pecans or walnuts)	¼	cup vegetable oil
¾	cup sweet shredded coconut	¾	teaspoon salt
¼	cup plus 2 tablespoons dark brown sugar	1	cup raisins

Preheat oven to 250°. In large bowl combine oats, nuts, coconut, and brown sugar. In separate bowl combine maple syrup, oil and salt. Combine both mixtures and pour onto 2 wax paper lined sheet pans. Bake for 1 hour stirring every 15 minutes to achieve an even color. Remove from oven and transfer to large bowl. Add raisins and mix well.

Yield: 6 to 8 servings

Easy Squeezy Cheesy Bars

2	(8-ounce) cans crescent rolls	1	cup sugar
2	(8-ounce) packages cream cheese, softened	1	teaspoon vanilla

TOPPING

½	cup sugar	1	teaspoon cinnamon

Preheat oven to 350°. Spray 9 x 13-inch baking pan with nonstick cooking spray. Unroll 1 package of crescent rolls in prepared pan, pinching seams together. Mix cream cheese, sugar and vanilla. Spread on top of crescent rolls in pan. Top with second package of crescent rolls, pinching seams together. Mix ½ cup of sugar with cinnamon and sprinkle over crescent rolls. Bake for 30 minutes or until nice and brown.

Yield: 12 servings

Banana Blueberry Bread

1½ cups all-purpose flour	½	cup sugar
1¼ teaspoons baking powder	⅓	cup vegetable oil
½ teaspoon baking soda	1	teaspoon vanilla
1 cup fresh or frozen blueberries	1	large egg
1½ ripe bananas, mashed		

Preheat oven to 350°. Spray 8 inch square pan with baking spray. Combine flour, baking powder and baking soda. Stir in blueberries. In another bowl, whisk remaining ingredients until smooth and add to flour mixture. Pour into pan and bake for 35 minutes.

Yield: 16 servings

Variation
Banana Cranberry Bread

Substitute fresh cranberries for blueberries.

Cinnamon Pull-Apart Bread

2   (7½-ounce) cans refrigerator
    buttermilk biscuits
¾   cup sugar

1   tablespoon ground cinnamon
½   cup butter or margarine,
    melted and divided

GLAZE
4   ounces cream cheese, softened
½   cup powdered sugar

2   tablespoons milk

Preheat oven to 350°. Grease 12 cup fluted tube pan. Cut biscuits into quarters with scissors. Mix sugar and cinnamon in medium bowl and roll dough quarters in sugar mixture. Place half of biscuits into pan. Drizzle with ¼ cup of melted butter. Top with remaining biscuit quarters and melted butter. Top loaf with remaining sugar mixture. Bake for 40 to 45 minutes or until golden. While bread is cooking prepare glaze by combining cream cheese and powdered sugar in bowl with an electric mixer blending well. Add 1 to 2 tablespoons of milk, beating until desired consistency. Remove baked bread from oven. Let loaf stand 5 minutes; invert onto plate. Spoon glaze over warm cake.

Yield: 1 large coffee cake

Corn Spoon Bread

1   small onion, sliced
¼   cup butter or margarine
1   (8½-ounce) package Jiffy corn
    muffin mix
1   cup (8 ounces) sour cream

2   eggs, beaten
1   (8-ounce) can creamed corn
1   (8-ounce) can whole corn,
    drained
1   cup grated Cheddar cheese

Preheat oven to 350°. Sauté onion in butter until clear in color. Mix corn muffin mix with sour cream, eggs, and both cans of corn. Pour into 9 x 13 inch casserole dish. Bake for 30 to 40 minutes (not completely done). Put cheese and onions on top and continue to cook until done (about 10 minutes more).

Yield: 8 to 10 servings

Historical Note: Spoon bread was a staple served at tables at the time of the Revolutionary War. It is a very rich and dense cornbread, so dense that it must be eaten with a spoon, and was a favorite of George Washington.

Blueberry Buckle

2 cups plus 2 tablespoons all-purpose flour, separated
2 teaspoons baking powder
½ teaspoons salt
¼ cup unsalted butter or margarine, softened

¾ cup sugar
1 egg
2 cups blueberries, fresh or frozen

Topping
¼ cup unsalted butter or margarine
½ cup sugar

⅓ cup all-purpose flour
½ teaspoon cinnamon

Preheat oven to 375°. Grease 9 x 13 inch pan. Mix together 2 cups of flour, baking powder and salt and set aside. Cream butter and sugar until fluffy, about 3 minutes. Beat in egg. Add flour mixture in 3 parts, alternating with milk. Gently fold blueberries into remaining 2 tablespoons of flour; separate and scatter evenly though out batter. Spread batter into prepared pan and set aside. Combine ingredients for topping with pastry cutter or fork to make crumbly mixture. Sprinkle topping over batter. Bake for 35 minutes or until toothpick comes out clean. Cool cake and lightly dust with powdered sugar.

Yield: 12 servings

Note: If using frozen blueberries do not thaw.

Mexican Cornbread

1½ cups self-rising cornmeal
3 eggs, beaten
1 cup creamed corn
1 cup buttermilk
⅔ cup oil
1 teaspoon salt

3 jalapeño peppers, seeded and chopped (wear rubber gloves) or canned peppers
1 medium onion, chopped
1 green pepper, chopped
1½ cups grated sharp Cheddar cheese
½ cup taco sauce

Preheat oven to 350°. Mix all ingredients together except cheese. Pour half cornmeal mixture into greased 9 x 13 inch baking dish. Sprinkle with cheese and cover with remaining mixture. Bake for 45 to 60 minutes.

Yield: 12 to 24 servings

Broccoli Cornbread

1 (8-ounce) box Jiffy cornbread mix

1 (10-ounce) package frozen chopped broccoli, thawed and drained

1 small onion, chopped

1 green onion, chopped

1 cup grated sharp Cheddar cheese

4 eggs, beaten

½ cup butter or margarine, melted

½ teaspoon salt

Preheat oven to 350°. Mix all ingredients in medium bowl and pour into greased glass pie pan. Bake for 45 minutes.

Yield: 8 servings

Variation
Spinach Cornbread

One (10-ounce) package frozen spinach, thawed and water squeezed out can be substituted for broccoli.

Historical Note: Cornbread is as Southern as grits and an absolute necessity with a good pot of greens. Legend has it that wheat was unavailable to Southerners during the Civil War (due to the Union blockade) but corn was a very common crop and, thus, became the grain of choice.

Strawberry Bread

3 cups all-purpose flour

1 teaspoon baking soda

1 teaspoon cinnamon

1 teaspoon salt

2 cups sugar

1½ cups vegetable oil

4 eggs, well beaten

2 (10-ounce) packages frozen strawberries, thawed and drained well

1 teaspoon red food coloring

Preheat oven to 350°. Grease and flour two 5 x 9 inch loaf pans. Mix flour, soda, cinnamon, salt, and sugar in large bowl. Make hole in center of flour mixture and pour in oil, beaten eggs and strawberries. Mix by hand until well blended. Add food coloring. Pour into loaf pans. Bake for 1 hour. Cool in pans for about 15 minutes. Remove and place on a wire rack to finish cooling.

Yield: 2 loaves

Pumpkin Bread

3½ cups all-purpose flour	2 teaspoons pumpkin pie spice
3 cups sugar	1 (16-ounce) can pumpkin
2 teaspoons baking soda	1 cup oil
1 teaspoon baking powder	4 eggs
3 teaspoons cinnamon	½ cup water

Preheat oven to 350°. Spray 2 large or 3 medium loaf pans with baking spray. Mix dry ingredients in large mixing bowl. Add remaining ingredients and beat thoroughly. Divide batter between loaf pans. Bake for approximately 1 hour 15 minutes.

Yield: 2 or 3 loaves

Variations
Pumpkin Date Bread
Add 1 (8-ounce) package chopped dates.

Pumpkin Cranberry Bread
Add 1 cup raisins, ½ (12-ounce) bag of fresh cranberries, and 1 cup chopped walnuts.

Six Week Bran Muffins

1 (15-ounce) box of raisin bran flakes	5 teaspoons baking soda
1 teaspoon salt	5 cups all-purpose flour
3 cups sugar	1 quart buttermilk
	4 eggs, beaten

Mix all ingredients and store in covered container in refrigerator for up to 6 weeks. When ready to use preheat oven to 350°. Fill greased muffin tins ¾ full. Bake for 15 minutes.

Yield: 4 dozen muffins

Note: A mixture of half raisin brand flakes and half All Bran can be used.

Scotch Scones with Orange Glaze

SCONES

¼ cup (½ stick) unsalted butter, chilled and cut into chunks

2 cups biscuit baking mix

1 egg

¾ cup milk or sour cream

½ cup sugar

¼ cup (½ stick) butter or margarine, melted

1 egg, beaten

GLAZE

2 tablespoons unsalted butter

2 cups sifted powdered sugar

2 oranges, juiced

Zest 1 orange

Preheat oven to 400°. Spray cookie sheet with cooking spray. In large bowl cut butter into baking mix using pastry blender. Butter pieces should be coated with biscuit mix and resemble crumbs. In small bowl mix milk and egg together: add sugar. Combine with biscuit mix and butter mixture to form dough. Mix just to incorporate, do not over work dough. Gently form dough into ball on floured board. Knead dough 5 times. Roll dough to ½ inch thickness. Cut into 2 inch squares, brush with melted butter. Fold each square into triangle, slightly seal edges by pinching. Triangles can be brushed with slightly beaten egg to add shine. Bake for 6 to 8 minutes or until golden brown. Cool on cookie sheet. Prepare glaze by combining butter, sugar, juice and orange zest in double boiler. Cook until butter and sugar are melted and mixture thickens. Remove from heat and beat until smooth and slightly cool. Drizzle or brush tops of cooled scones. Let glaze get hazy and harden before serving.

Yield: 18 scones

Variations

Cranberry Scones

Coarsely chop 1½ cups of fresh cranberries and place in small bowl. Add 1 cup sugar and mix. Sit over night. Add to scone mixture. Scones will turn somewhat red. Adjust sugar to taste.

Scotch Scones Variations continued

Blueberry Scones

Add 1½ cups of fresh blueberries to scone mixture. If using frozen blueberries, coat with 2 tablespoons of flour before adding to scone mixture.

Historical Note: Scones are Scottish quick breads said to have taken the name from the Stone of Destiny (or Scone), the place where Scottish kings were once crowned. Originally triangular-shaped, they were made with oats and griddle-baked.

Apple Carrot Muffins

2 cups all-purpose flour	1 large peeled chopped Granny Smith apple
1 cup sugar	
2 teaspoons baking soda	½ cup raisins
2 teaspoons cinnamon	3 eggs, room temperature
½ teaspoon salt	⅔ cup canola oil
2 cups shredded carrots	½ cup chopped walnuts

Preheat oven to 350°. Grease muffin pans and set aside. Combine flour, sugar, baking soda, cinnamon and salt in large mixing bowl; mix well. Add carrots, apples, raisins, and walnuts; stir well. Beat eggs, add oil. Add to dry ingredients and stir to mix just until dry ingredients are moistened. Spoon batter into prepared muffin pans filling two thirds full. Bake for 20 to 25 minutes or until golden and a wooden pick comes out clean. Do not over cook. Remove pans to wire rack to cool.

Yield: 18 medium muffins

Note: Muffins freeze well.

Rosemary Biscuits

1 (3-ounce) package cream cheese

1¾ cups biscuit mix

½ cup milk

2 teaspoons fresh snipped rosemary

Preheat oven to 400°. Cut cream cheese into biscuit mix until crumbly. Add milk and rosemary until just moistened. Turn out on lightly floured surface and knead 3 or 4 times. Roll dough to ¾ inch thickness. Cut with biscuit cutter. Place on cookie sheet and bake for 10 minutes or until lightly browned.

Yield: 8 to 10 biscuits

Cheddar Drop Biscuits

2 cups biscuit baking mix

⅔ cup milk

½ cup (2 ounces) grated Cheddar cheese

¼ cup (½ stick) butter or margarine, melted

¼ teaspoon garlic powder

Preheat oven to 450°. Grease cookie sheet. Combine biscuit mix, milk and cheese; beat with wooden spoon for about 30 seconds. Drop by spoonfuls onto prepared cookie sheet. Smooth tops down with a spoon. Bake for 8 to 10 minutes. Combine butter and garlic powder and pour over hot biscuits.

Yield: 8 servings

Historical Note: It is believed that the popular "biscuit" evolved from the English scone, which requires butter and eggs. Settlers seldom had these, substituted lard for butter, omitted the eggs and what came out of the oven was a biscuit.

Salads, Slaws
Soups & Stews

Isle of Hope's Original Plantations

In 1736, three years after Oglethorpe arrived in Savannah, three men each received a grant of 500 acres and established plantations on the Isle of Hope. Noble Jones, a long time friend of Oglethorpe, was an English surveyor and carpenter who was first hired to survey the people's lots in Savannah and later served as a constable or bailiff. Along with his wife, Sarah, and two children, Noble Wimberley and Mary, he established a plantation he named Wormsloe on the south side of the island. The land was leased and approval had to come from the trustees in London. After waiting nine years with no word, his request was resubmitted and finally approved in 1745. Wormsloe was never intended to be an agricultural plantation run for revenue, but rather, a country residence with planting of secondary importance.

The middle 500 acres were leased to John Fallowfield, a naval officer, who arrived in Savannah about a month after Noble Jones with specific plans to establish a plantation. He immediately began to clear land and his first year produced 95 bushels of Indian corn, 40 bushels of potatoes and 22 bushels of rice. He rented out his house in Savannah and lived most of the time on his plantation with his wife, Elizabeth, and three small children. He later became a dissident because of the restrictive rules of the colony and led a revolt against Oglethorpe, after which he left Savannah for Charleston, South Carolina in 1742. His land was eventually included in a royal grant to Noble Jones.

Henry Parker, a linen draper who also served as a bailiff in Savannah, was the third of the original Isle of Hope owners, having leased 500 acres on the northern end of the island. He rose from Third Bailiff to First Bailiff to President of the Council, therefore acting as governor of the colony. After his death, his wife, Ann, received the land as a grant for her and her heirs from Governor Henry Ellis on September 30, 1757. Though his plantation had been divided into numerous lots over the years, part of this area is still known today as Parkersburg.

Salad Dressings

Fruit Salads

Vegetable Salads and Slaws

Salads with Meat or Seafood

Pasta Salads

Soups and Stews

Shallot Balsamic Salad Dressing

1 medium shallot	2 teaspoons sugar
½ cup olive oil	¼ teaspoon salt
3 tablespoons balsamic vinegar	Freshly ground black pepper
1 tablespoon Dijon mustard	

Drop shallot into running food processor. Add remaining ingredients and mix.

Yield: 1 cup

Dressing for Spinach Salad

1 cup oil	2 tablespoons sugar
5 tablespoons red wine vinegar	Coarsely ground black pepper
4 tablespoons sour cream	2 tablespoons chopped parsley
1½ teaspoons salt	2 cloves garlic, crushed
½ teaspoon dry mustard	

Mix all ingredients and let stand for 6 hours.

Yield: 1½ cups

Blueberry Spinach Salad

1 shallot, chopped	1 (10-ounce) package fresh spinach, torn in bite size pieces
½ cup oil	
¼ cup raspberry vinegar	
2 teaspoons Dijon mustard	1 (4-ounce) package blue cheese, crumbled
1 teaspoon sugar	
½ teaspoon salt	1 cup fresh blueberries
	½ cup chopped pecans, toasted

Combine first 6 ingredients in jar and shake well. Toss spinach, blue cheese, blueberries and pecans. Add dressing and toss gently. Serve immediately.

Yield: 6 to 8 servings

Cranberry Salad Mold

2   cups hot water
2   (3-ounce) packages strawberry
      or raspberry gelatin
1   (16-ounce) can whole berry
      cranberry sauce

1   (12-ounce) package frozen
      strawberries or raspberries
1   cup sour cream at room
      temperature

Dissolve fruit gelatin in hot water. Add cranberry sauce and frozen strawberries or raspberries; chill until slightly set. Stir in sour cream so it looks marbleized. Chill in slightly greased mold until firm. Chopped apples and/or crushed pineapple and/or chopped pecans can also be added.

Yield: 12 servings

Grape Salad

1   (8-ounce) package cream
      cheese, softened
½   cup mayonnaise
⅓   cup sour cream
4   tablespoons sugar

1½ cups chopped nuts
5-6 cups seedless grapes, red and
      green
Brown sugar

Mix cream cheese, mayonnaise, sour cream, sugar, and nuts. Toss with grapes. Sprinkle with brown sugar.

Yield: 6 to 8 servings

Pineapple Orange Salad Mold

1   (20-ounce) can crushed
      pineapple

1   (6-ounce) package orange
      gelatin
2   cups buttermilk

Drain pineapple and save juice. Make gelatin according to package directions using reserved juice and water if needed. Stir until dissolved; add crushed pineapple then stir in buttermilk. Pour into greased mold and chill.

Yield: 8 servings

Mandarin Orange Salad

GARNISH

½ cup slivered almonds   3 tablespoons sugar

DRESSING

½ teaspoon salt   Chopped parsley
⅛ teaspoon freshly ground   2 tablespoons sugar
   pepper   2 tablespoons red wine vinegar
¼ cup olive oil   2-4 drops Tabasco sauce

SALAD

1 head iceberg lettuce, chopped   2 celery stalks, thinly sliced
   or torn into bite-size pieces   4 green onions, chopped
1 head romaine lettuce, chopped   1 (11-ounce) can Mandarin
   or torn into bite-size pieces   oranges, drained

Cook almonds slowly in dry skillet with sugar. Allow to cool. Mix dressing ingredients well. Mix salad ingredients together, toss with dressing, and garnish with almonds.

Yield: 6 servings

Watermelon Salad

3 tablespoons thinly sliced fresh   1 (4-pound) seedless watermelon,
   basil   cut into cubes (6 cups)
2 tablespoons fresh lime juice   ½ pound ricotta salata (salted dry
2 tablespoons extra-virgin olive   ricotta cheese), cut into
   oil   ¼ inch cubes
   Salt and pepper   ¼ cup pine nuts, toasted

Whisk first 3 ingredients in small bowl. Season dressing with salt and pepper to taste. Place watermelon and salata in medium serving bowl. Drizzle with dressing, toss and sprinkle with pine nuts.

Yield: 6 servings

Note: Salata is available at specialty food stores. Crumbled feta or cubed mozzarella can be substituted for salata.

Strawberry Spinach Salad

DRESSING

2 tablespoons lemon juice

2 tablespoons white vinegar

⅓ cup sugar

1 tablespoon vegetable oil

½ teaspoon lemon zest

1 teaspoon poppy seeds

SALAD

1 (6-ounce) package baby spinach or other lettuce

8 ounces fresh strawberries, quartered

1 cup sliced cucumber

¼ cup chopped Vidalia onion

¼ cup broken pecans, toasted and cooled

Mix all dressing ingredients together and chill. Layer spinach, strawberries, cucumber and onion. Pour dressing over and toss; then sprinkle with pecans.

Yield: 4 to 6 servings

Crunchy Broccoli Slaw

2 (12-ounce) packages broccoli slaw mix

1 cup regular or light mayonnaise

⅓ cup sugar

2 tablespoons cider vinegar

1 small red onion, chopped

½-¾ cup dried cranberries (Craisins) or raisins

¼ cup bacon, cooked and crumbled

½ cup chopped pecans, toasted (optional)

Rinse broccoli slaw mix with cold water and drain well. Stir together mayonnaise, sugar and vinegar in large bowl. Add slaw, onion and dried cranberries, tossing gently to coat. Cover and chill for 8 hours. Sprinkle with bacon and pecans just before serving.

Yield: 8 to 10 servings

Aunt Jo's Slaw

1 cup vegetable oil
2 teaspoons seasoned salt
1 teaspoon pepper
1-2 tablespoons sugar
6 tablespoons cider vinegar
1 (16-ounce) package coleslaw
1 bunch green onions chopped

1 (3¾-ounce) package sunflower seeds
1 (2¼-ounce) package slivered almonds
1 (3-ounce) package Ramen noodles, broken into small pieces (discard broth packet)

Combine first 5 ingredients in jar and shake. Toss remaining ingredients with dressing and serve.

Yield: 8 servings

Cucumber Salad Mold

1 (3-ounce) package lime gelatin
¾ cup hot water
¼ cup lemon juice
1 teaspoon onion juice

1 cup mayonnaise
1 cup peeled and chopped cucumber

Dissolve gelatin in hot water, add lemon juice and onion juice. Chill until partially set. Stir in mayonnaise and cucumber. Pour into mold. Chill until set. Center may be filled with shrimp or crabmeat.

Yield: 8 servings

Historical Note: For many years manufacturers experimented with making an appealing looking gelatin made from animal bones. Unfortunately it looked bad and tasted awful, so they solved the problem by adding fruit syrups. This new product was called Jello.

Marinated Greek Tomato Salad

6	medium tomatoes, sliced	½	cup red wine vinegar
¼	pound feta cheese, crumbled	2	tablespoons minced parsley
1	onion, thinly sliced	4	teaspoons sugar
1½	(6-ounce) cans pitted ripe olives, sliced	½	teaspoon shredded basil
		¼	teaspoon salt
½	cup olive oil	¼	teaspoon cracked black pepper

At least 3 hours before serving: place tomato slices, feta cheese, onion slices and olives in 9 x 13 inch baking dish. Mix olive oil, vinegar, parsley, sugar, basil, salt and pepper. Pour over tomato mixture. Cover and refrigerate.

Yield: 8 to 10 servings

Gourmet Marinated Salad

MARINADE

1	cup red wine vinegar	½	teaspoon dried thyme
½	cup vegetable oil	½	teaspoon dried oregano
1	garlic clove, crushed	1	teaspoon dried parsley
1½	teaspoons salt	2	tablespoons sugar
½	teaspoon freshly ground black pepper		

SALAD

1	purple onion, cut into rings	1	can hearts of palm, drained and cut in bite-size pieces
1	pound fresh mushrooms, sliced		
2	cans artichoke hearts, halved and drained	1	pint cherry or grape tomatoes
		1	can pitted black olives, drained
			Lettuce to garnish

Combine marinade ingredients in large bowl and mix well. Add all vegetables and toss with marinade. Cover and chill 24 hours. Drain and serve on lettuce. Sliced yellow squash, zucchini and/or broccoli may also be added.

Yield: 6 servings, but may vary depending upon the amount of vegetables used

Molded Gazpacho Salad with Avocado Dressing

SALAD MOLD

2 (¼-ounce) envelopes unflavored gelatin
1 (18-ounce) can tomato juice, divided
⅓ cup red wine vinegar or balsamic vinegar
1 teaspoon salt

1 teaspoon Tabasco sauce
1 cup peeled tomato, diced
1 cup peeled cucumber, diced
½ cup diced green pepper
¼ cup finely chopped red onion
1 tablespoon chopped chives

DRESSING

1 large ripe avocado, peeled and pitted
½ cup sour cream
½ cup light cream
1 tablespoon grated onion

¾ teaspoon salt
⅛ teaspoon pepper
⅛ teaspoon sugar
1 clove garlic, crushed
1 tablespoon lemon juice

In medium saucepan, soften gelatin in ¾ cup tomato juice. Dissolve over low heat, stirring constantly. Remove from heat. Stir in remaining tomato juice, vinegar, salt and Tabasco. Set pan in bowl of ice water; stir until mixture thickens. Fold in tomato, cucumber, green pepper, onion and chives. Pour into 1½ cup mold that has been rinsed with cold water. Chill 6 hours until firm. Combine all dressing ingredients in blender or food processor and mix until smooth. Chill. When ready to serve, unmold salad on platter and serve with dressing. (Guacamole, thinned with sour cream, can be substituted for dressing.)

Yield: 10 servings

Black Bean and Corn Salad

1 (15-ounce) can black beans, rinsed and drained

2 cups fresh or thawed frozen corn

2 jalapeño peppers, seeded and finely chopped (wear plastic gloves when handling)

2 plum tomatoes, seeded and chopped

½ cup finely chopped red onion

2 cloves garlic, minced

¼ cup chopped fresh cilantro

2 tablespoons lime juice

1 tablespoon olive oil

2 teaspoons Southwest-style seasoning mix

¼ teaspoon salt

Combine beans, corn, peppers, tomatoes, onion, garlic and cilantro. Mix lime juice, oil, seasoning mix and salt. Pour over salad. Cover and refrigerate for at lest 1 hour to allow flavors to develop.

Yield: 4 servings

Southwestern Cornbread Salad

1 (6-ounce) package Mexican cornbread mix; cooked, cooled and crumbled

1 head Romaine lettuce (or mixed salad greens), chopped

2 large tomatoes, chopped

1 (15-ounce) can black beans, drained and rinsed

1 (15-ounce) can corn with red and green pepper, drained

1 (8-ounce) package shredded Mexican four cheese blend

6 slices bacon, cooked and crumbled

5 green onions, chopped

1 (1-ounce) envelope Hidden Valley ranch dressing mix, prepared according to directions

In large bowl, layer half each of cornbread and lettuce and next 6 ingredients, Top with half dressing. Repeat. Cover and chill at least 2 hours.

Yield: 10 to 12 servings

Sour Cream Potato Salad

6	cups warm potatoes, cooked and diced	4	hard-boiled eggs, chopped
1	teaspoon salt	½	cup mayonnaise
⅓	cup Italian salad dressing	½	cup sour cream
1	cup diced celery	1	tablespoon horseradish
⅓	cup sliced green onions	2	teaspoons mustard

Sprinkle warm potatoes with salt; drizzle with Italian dressing. Chill 2 hours. Add celery, onion and eggs. Combine mayonnaise, sour cream, horseradish and mustard; carefully fold into salad.

Yield: 8 servings

Asparagus, Shrimp and Orange Salad

SALAD

2	pounds asparagus, trimmed	1	pound shrimp, cooked, peeled and deveined
½	cup plus 2 tablespoons fresh chopped chives, divided		Salt and pepper
3	navel oranges		

DRESSING

3	tablespoons fresh orange juice	1	teaspoon grated orange peel
3	tablespoons sugar	¼	cup Dijon mustard
2	tablespoons distilled white vinegar		Salt and pepper

Cook asparagus in large pot of boiling salted water until crisp-tender, about 4 minutes. Cut top 5 inches of asparagus and set aside for garnish. Slice remaining asparagus into ¼ inch thick rounds. Transfer slices into large bowl and mix in ½ cup chives. Cut and peel white pith from oranges. Working over bowl, cut between membranes to release segments. Drain off juices. Transfer segments to bowl with asparagus and chives. Gently mix in shrimp. Add salt and pepper to taste. For dressing, whisk fresh orange juice, sugar, vinegar and orange peel until sugar dissolves. Whisk in mustard. Add salt and pepper to taste. Divide asparagus stalks among 6 plates and mound salad in center of plates. Pour dressing over each salad. Sprinkle with remaining 2 tablespoons chives. Refrigerated orange slices or Mandarin oranges can be substituted for navel oranges as well as crabmeat for shrimp.

Yield: 6 servings

Chicken Pasta Salad

1 (6-ounce) package corkscrew pasta	1 tablespoon mustard
	¾ cup sliced black olives
3 cups cooked chicken breast, diced	1 cup diced cucumber or zucchini
½ cup Italian salad dressing	1 cup diced celery
½ cup mayonnaise	Salt and pepper
3 tablespoons lemon juice	

Cook pasta according to package directions. While still hot, mix pasta with chicken and salad dressing. Let cool. Blend mayonnaise, mustard and lemon juice; set aside. Add vegetables and olives to chicken mixture. Add mayonnaise mixture and stir thoroughly. Add salt and pepper to taste. Chill at least 2 hours.

Yield: 6 servings

Chicken Waldorf Salad
with Dates and Caramelized Pine Nuts

1½ tablespoons sugar	½ cup chopped dates
1½ teaspoons Balsamic vinegar	¼ cup mayonnaise
⅓ cup pine nuts	3 tablespoons plain yogurt
2 cups cooked chicken, diced	Lettuce
1 tart apple, peeled and chopped	

Preheat oven to 325°. Spray small baking dish with nonstick spray. Combine sugar and vinegar in small saucepan; dissolve over medium heat, about 2 minutes. Add nuts and toss to coat completely. Place in baking dish and bake for 8 to 10 minutes, stirring occasionally until brown. Set aside. Combine chicken, apple and dates in bowl. Mix mayonnaise and yogurt in separate bowl. Pour over chicken mixture. Toss to coat all ingredients. Serve over lettuce and sprinkle with nuts.

Yield: 4 servings

Chutney Chicken Salad

1 cup mayonnaise
½ cup Major Grey Chutney
8 chicken breast halves, cooked and chopped
2 stalks celery, coarsely chopped

1 Granny Smith apple, unpeeled and chopped (sprinkled with lemon juice)
½ cup sliced red seedless grapes
½ cup chopped pecans, toasted
2 cups cooked brown rice
2 onions, chopped

Thoroughly blend mayonnaise and chutney. Combine with remaining ingredients. Serve chilled.

Yield: 6 servings

Variation
Cranberry Chicken Salad
Omit chutney and grapes. Add ¾ cup dried cranberries.

Curried Chicken and Rice Salad

1½ cups cooked rice
¼ cup minced onion
2 tablespoons salad oil
1 tablespoon vinegar
2 teaspoons curry powder

1 cup diced celery
1 (10-ounce) box frozen peas, thawed
2 cups cooked chicken, chopped
¾ cup mayonnaise

Blend all ingredients and refrigerate at least 3 hours. Sprinkle with additional curry before serving. Keeps well for several days. Good with fresh fruit and rolls. Also good stuffed in tomato.

Yield: 8 servings

Variation
Curried Shrimp and Rice Salad
Substitute 2 cups of shrimp for chicken.

Hawaiian Chicken Salad

2½ cups cooked chicken, diced
1 (20-ounce) can pineapple
   tidbits, drained
1 cup halved seedless red grapes
¾ cup diced celery
¾ cup mayonnaise
½ teaspoon salt
¼ teaspoon pepper
1 cup navel orange sections
1 sliced firm banana
⅓ cup salted peanuts

Combine first 7 ingredients. Fold in oranges. Cover and refrigerate until chilled. Just before serving, fold in bananas and sprinkle with peanuts.

Yield: 8 servings

Wonderful Tuna Salad

1 (12-ounce) can water-packed
   solid white tuna, drained
⅓ cup (3 ounces) plain yogurt or
   mayonnaise
1 (4-ounce) can crushed
   pineapple, drained
1 celery rib, finely chopped
¼ cup sweet pickle relish
¼ cup chopped pecans
1 teaspoon mustard
⅛ teaspoon ground cinnamon

Mix all ingredients together. Don't let the pineapple throw you; it's delicious.

Yield: 4 servings

Broccoli Almond Pasta Salad

½ pound fusilli pasta
½ cup oil
½ cup cider vinegar
2 tablespoons sesame oil
1 cloves garlic, minced
   Florets from large bunch
   broccoli, chopped
1 (2¼-ounce) package sliced
   almonds, toasted
4 slices bacon, cooked and
   crumbled
2 green onions, chopped
½ cup grated Parmesan cheese

Cook fusilli pasta according to package instructions. Drain and rinse with cool water. Combine oil, vinegar, sesame oil and garlic in large jar. Mix well. Toss pasta and dressing with remaining ingredients. Chill overnight.

Yield: 8 to 10 servings

Basmati Rice Salad with Peas

2¼ cups water
½ teaspoon salt
1½ cups basmati rice, uncooked
1 (10-ounce) box frozen baby peas, defrosted, not cooked
¼ cup sliced green onions with some green tops
¼ cup fresh coarsely chopped dill
½ cup mayonnaise
2 teaspoons onion powder
1 tablespoon white vinegar
Salt and pepper

Bring water and salt to boil. Rinse rice in strainer and add to water. Reduce heat to low; cover and cook until water is absorbed and rice is tender, about 20 minutes. Remove from heat and let stand 5 minutes. Fluff with fork and let cool. Mix peas, green onions, dill, mayonnaise, onion powder and vinegar with rice. Add salt and pepper to taste. Serve chilled or at room temperature on platter garnished with greens.

Yield: 8 servings

Crunchy Asian Salad

DRESSING
1 cup oil
3 tablespoons soy sauce
⅓-½ cup sugar
½ cup wine vinegar

SALAD
1 cup chopped walnuts
1 (3-ounce) package Ramen noodles broken into bite-size pieces (discard flavor packet)
4 tablespoons butter
4 green onions, sliced
1 bunch broccoli, chopped
1 head Romaine lettuce or 2 hearts, sliced or chopped

Combine all dressing ingredients up to 2 days ahead. Sauté walnuts and noodles in butter the day before. Cool, drain and store in zip bag. In large bowl, place broccoli, onions and lettuce. Just before serving, add dressing and walnut mixture. Toss to coat.

Yield: 8 to 10 servings

Brunswick Stew for a Crowd

2   pounds ground chuck
1   onion, diced
1   (10-ounce) can Castleberry BBQ Chicken, Beef or Pork
1   (9¾-ounce) can chicken or cooked chicken, diced
2   (15-ounce) cans creamed corn
2   (16-ounce) cans crushed tomatoes

1   (16-ounce) bag frozen mixed vegetables
1   cup mustard based BBQ sauce
¼   cup Worcestershire sauce
1   cup strong black coffee
1   (16-ounce) bag frozen butter beans
    Salt and pepper
¼   cup liquid smoke (optional)

Brown ground chuck with onion. Drain well and mix with all other ingredients in very large pot. Simmer 2 to 3 hours on very low heat.

Yield: 20 to 24 servings

Historical Note: Brunswick stew probably originated in Brunswick County, Virginia (not Brunswick, Georgia) when a member of the state legislature asked his camp cook to prepare stew for friends in 1828.

Cream of Broccoli Soup

6   cups water
4   chicken bouillon cubes
1   medium onion chopped
3   (10-ounce) boxes frozen chopped broccoli
1   teaspoon each of salt and pepper
1   cup milk

1   cup half-and-half
½   cup butter or margarine, melted
½   cup all-purpose flour
½   cup water
1   pound Velveeta, cut into small cubes

In 4 quart pot, combine first 5 ingredients and cook until onions and broccoli are tender. Add milk and half-and-half. Mix together butter, flour and water and stir into soup. Add Velveeta and stir until cheese is melted.

Yield: 10 to 12 servings

Variation
Oyster Broccoli Stew

Cook 2 pints undrained oysters in another saucepan until edges curl. Add to soup mixture and serve.

Chicken and Shrimp Gumbo

½ cup butter or margarine
2 medium onions, chopped (2 cups)
1 red pepper, chopped
2 ribs celery, chopped
2 cloves garlic, minced
½ cup all-purpose flour
2 (14½-ounce) cans chicken broth
1 (14½-ounce) can diced tomatoes
1 teaspoon salt
½ teaspoon pepper
4 boneless, skinless chicken thighs cut into ¾ inch pieces
1 cup frozen cut okra
½ pound large shrimp, peeled and deveined
½ teaspoon hot pepper sauce

In large pot, melt butter; add onions, red pepper, celery and garlic. Cook, stirring constantly, until onion is softened (5 to 6 minutes). Stir in flour and cook until slightly brown, about 5 minutes. Stir in broth, tomatoes with juice, salt and pepper. Bring to boil. Add chicken. Reduce heat and cook 10 minutes. Add okra; cook 5 minutes. Add shrimp; cook until pink. Stir in hot sauce. Serve "as is" or over hot cooked rice.

Yield: 6 servings

GUMBO

Gumbo is a spicy, hearty stew or soup, typically found in the South. It is more commonly served in colder months due to the extended cooking time required, as a large pot of simmering gumbo will heat up the surrounding area. Okra, filé powder and roux are common thickening agents.

Mexican Corn Chowder

3 tablespoons butter
4 boneless chicken breasts, cubed (1½ pounds)
1 small onion, chopped
2 cloves garlic, minced
2 cups half-and-half
2 cups shredded Monterey Jack cheese
2 (14½-ounce) cans creamed corn
1 (4½-ounce) can chopped green chilies, undrained
½ teaspoon hot sauce
¼ teaspoon salt
1 teaspoon cumin
2 tablespoons chopped fresh cilantro

Melt butter in stockpot. Add chicken, onion and garlic and sauté 10 minutes. Stir in other ingredients and cook 15 minutes, stirring often. Stir in cilantro.

Yield: 8 servings

Driftaway Crab Stew

4	tablespoons butter or margarine	1	(10 ½-ounce) can Campbell's Cream of Celery Soup
½	small onion, diced	1	cup heavy cream
2	ribs celery, chopped	1	pound fresh or pasteurized crabmeat
1	tablespoon seafood seasoning		
	Pinch cayenne		Chopped green onion for garnish
1	cup all-purpose flour		
2-3 cups water			Shredded cheeses for garnish
1	tablespoon crab base or seafood bouillon		Sherry

In soup pot, melt butter and sauté onions and celery over medium heat for 5 to 7 minutes. Add seafood seasoning and cayenne pepper and sauté an additional 2 minutes. Add flour and whisk until well blended. Add enough water, whisking vigorously, until desired consistency of slightly thickened roux/gravy. Add crab base and continue stirring over medium heat until almost boiling. Add cream of celery soup and continue whisking until boiling. Whisk in cream until blended. Remove from heat and gently fold in crabmeat. Serve hot, sprinkled with your choice of green onions, shredded cheeses or drizzled with sherry. Very thick soup. If thinner consistency is desired, use less flour

Yield: 6 to 8 servings

Note: This recipe, from the Driftaway Café in Sand Fly, has been revised for the home cook.

CANNED SOUPS: A STAPLE IN METHODIST COOKING

Historical Note: The Campbell Soup Company was started in 1869 and is deeply ingrained in American history. The invention of condensed soup in 1897 was a huge success, making it possible to offer a ten ounce can for only a dime. Tomato soup was introduced the same year, while cream of mushroom and chicken noodle first appeared in 1934. Combined, Americans consume approximately 2.5 billion bowls of these three soups alone each year.

Italian Sausage Tortellini Soup

1 pound sweet Italian sausage (link)
2 (10-ounce) cans condensed French onion soup
1 (14-ounce) can stewed tomatoes
2 cups shredded cabbage (or slaw mix), or zucchini
6 cups water
1 teaspoon dried basil
2 cups cheese tortellini (about 1 package)
Salt and pepper
Grated Parmesan cheese

Remove casing from sausage and break into small pieces. Brown and drain. Add soup, tomatoes, cabbage, water and basil; bring to boil and simmer 30 minutes. Add tortellini and cook 15 minutes more. Correct seasonings. Top with Parmesan cheese and serve with crusty French bread to dip.

Yield: 6 to 8 servings

Oyster Brie Soup

1 cup (2 sticks) butter or margarine
½ cup diced celery
½ cup diced onion
½ teaspoon salt
½ teaspoon white pepper
½ teaspoon cayenne pepper
½ cup all-purpose flour
3 cups cold water
1 cup heavy cream
¼ cup champagne or dry white wine
2 tablespoons sherry
1 tablespoon crab or seafood base (optional)
16 ounces oysters, undrained
18 ounces Brie cheese, in wedges, no skin

Melt butter and add celery, onions, salt, pepper and cayenne. Cook until vegetables begin to soften. Add flour to make roux. Whisk on low heat until has nutty smell; at least 10 minutes. Slowly add water while whisking. Add cream and wines; simmer about 5 minutes. Add oysters and slowly add Brie while whisking until fully incorporated.

Yield: 8 servings

Roasted Tomato Basil Soup

3	pounds fresh ripe plum tomatoes, halved	2	tablespoons unsalted butter
¼	cup plus 2 tablespoons good quality olive oil	¼	teaspoon crushed red pepper flakes
1	tablespoon kosher salt	1	(28-ounce) can plum tomatoes, with juice
1½	teaspoons black pepper, freshly ground	1	cup shredded fresh basil leaves
2	cups chopped yellow onions	1	teaspoon fresh thyme leaves
6	cloves garlic, minced	1	quart chicken stock or water
			Salt and pepper

Preheat oven to 400°. Toss together fresh tomatoes, ¼ cup olive oil, salt and pepper. Spread tomatoes in 1 layer on baking sheet and roast for 45 minutes. In 8 quart stockpot over medium heat, sauté onions and garlic with 2 tablespoons olive oil, butter and red pepper flakes 10 minutes, until onions start to brown. Add canned tomatoes, basil, thyme, and chicken stock. Add oven roasted tomatoes, including liquid on baking sheet. Bring to boil and simmer uncovered 40 minutes. Pass through food mill fitted with coarsest blade. Add salt and pepper. Serve hot or cold.

Yield: 6 to 8 servings

EASY GAZPACHO FROM LEFTOVERS
Don't throw out leftover tossed green salad. Save and toss it in the blender with some tomato juice for a few seconds. Refrigerate. Voila! Gazpacho for lunch the next day.

Southwestern Soup

1 large onion, chopped
4 tablespoons butter
1⅓ cups raw white rice
3 quarts chicken broth
1 teaspoon cumin
2 cans (15½-ounce) garbanzo
   beans, undrained
2 cans (14½-ounce) gold or white
   hominy, undrained

2 cups cooked chicken or turkey,
   diced
2 cans (4-ounce) diced green
   chilies
Salt and pepper
Lime wedges
Monterey Jack cheese, grated
Chopped cilantro and paprika
   for garnish

Sauté onions in butter for 5 minutes. Add rice and sauté until rice is opaque. Put rice mixture into large soup pot; add broth, cumin, garbanzo beans, hominy, chicken and diced green chilies. Cook 20 minutes. Add salt and pepper to taste. Serve with lime wedges and grated cheese. Sprinkle with cilantro and paprika. Warm tortillas go great with this soup!

Yield: 12 to 16 servings

VEGETABLE SOUP FROM LEFTOVERS

Place all leftover vegetables with the liquid in which they were cooked, in a freezer container. When full, add tomato juice or a can of tomatoes, seasoning and leftover chopped meat if desired to create a quick and easy soup.

Marvelous Meats
& Marinades

Day on the Island: A Special Tradition

In 1969, a group of women in the church realized the need for more fellowship, as well as a way to earn money for some improvements to the church. They put their heads together and came up with the idea of a special day on the Isle of Hope. The first Day on the Island was an antique tea in one of the lovely homes on the bluff. The following year, they decided on a river cruise and lunch but, unfortunately, the weather did not co-operate. It poured buckets, so this idea was not repeated.

In 1972, the Day on the Island consisted of a bazaar, tour of homes and a chicken salad lunch. This format was a huge success and has been used ever since. The women worked in small groups all year making items to sell in the bazaar and fellowship flourished as they planned and worked together. Each year, the bazaar and the crafts grew larger and more elaborate so that a number of Sunday School rooms were needed to display the finished products. There was a plant shop, hospitality room and shops selling baked goods and holiday decorations of all types. In addition, a silent auction was held that grew to include several hundred donated items by 2004. The luncheon menu remained the same over the thirty years and people looked forward to that wonderful hot chicken salad, spiced peaches and trifle. The women prepared for and served about 2,000 people each Day on the Island.

In recent years, Day on the Island has become a biannual event because of the time and effort required. The women continue to work together in small groups, stressing the importance of Christian fellowship.

Each year, the profits from the Day on the Island festivities have increased. During the first year, 90% of the money earned went to pay for improvements in the church and 10% was given to missions. Gradually, however, that changed. Currently, almost all of the profits from the bazaar, luncheon and tour are spent on missions, with much of the money donated to special needs in the Savannah community. The members of the Isle of Hope United Methodist Church firmly believe in the Wesleyan tradition of lending a helping hand to any in need.

Day of the Island Chairs

1969-71	Carolyn Solana	1979	Emily Saussy	1994	Pat Royal
1972	Joan Broerman	1980	Ruth Quattlebaum	1996	Julie Vann
1973	Gary Curlee	1981	Nancy Hughes	1998	Nancy Fuqua
1974	Nancy Hartmann	1982	Kay Monroe	2000	Shirley Grotheer
1975	Kay Monroe	1984	Tricia Windom	2002	Judy Walker
1976	Sarah Nettles	1986	Mary Tom Byram	2004	Johnnie Morris
1977	Libby Lindsey	1988	Carole Beason	2006	Mimi Jones
1978	Barbara Andrews	1990	Debbie Nash		Katherine Slagel
		1992	Margaret Callaway		

Beef

Pork

Lamb

Veal

Marinated Filet Mignon

6   small filet mignons (about 1¾ to 2 inches thick)

MARINADE

½   cup olive oil
1   clove garlic, crushed

2   teaspoons finely fresh rosemary
2   teaspoons finely chopped fresh thyme

TOPPING

2   tablespoons butter or margarine

1   teaspoon Worcestershire sauce
1   teaspoon Dijon mustard

Place filets in plastic zip bag. Combine olive oil, garlic, rosemary and thyme in bowl or measuring cup. Pour over meat, seal bag and refrigerate 1 to 24 hours. While steaks are marinating, mix together butter, Worcestershire and mustard. Refrigerate. Place meat over hot coals and grill about 10 minutes per side, or until internal temperature reaches 140 to 150° (medium rare). Remove filets to warm platter. Place 1 teaspoon flavored butter on top of each filet.

Yield: 6 servings

Peppered Steak with Merlot Glaze

Black pepper, freshly ground
2   T-bone, sirloin, or other tender cuts of beef

3   tablespoons butter or margarine, divided
⅓   cup Merlot (or other dry red wine)

Several hours before serving, season steaks with cracked pepper and allow to rest in refrigerator. Return steaks to room temperature before cooking. Heat black iron skillet until very hot, add 1 tablespoon butter and steaks. Reduce heat to medium and cook for 4 minutes. Turn steaks and cook another 3 minutes. Remove steaks and add 2 tablespoons butter and ⅓ cup Merlot. Reduce to glaze and pour over steaks.

Yield: 2 servings

Steak San Marco

2 pounds chuck steak, round steak, pork chop or other meat
1 envelope onion soup mix
1 tablespoon dried oregano
Dash of garlic powder
2 tablespoons vinegar
2 tablespoons oil
1 (14-ounce) can diced tomatoes

Cut meat into serving size pieces and place in skillet. Sprinkle with soup, oregano, garlic, vinegar and oil. Spread tomatoes over meat. Cover and simmer 1½ hours or until tender. Good served over rice.

Yields: 6 servings

Grilled London Broil

2 pounds flank steak or good top round steak cut for London Broil (use with one of the following marinades)

SOY GINGER MARINADE

¼ cup soy sauce
3 tablespoons honey
2 tablespoons wine vinegar
1½ teaspoons garlic salt
1½ teaspoons ginger

BALSAMIC HERB MARINADE

¼ cup balsamic vinegar
⅓ cup olive oil
1 tablespoon shredded fresh basil
1 teaspoon fresh thyme
1 teaspoon chopped fresh rosemary
1 teaspoon minced garlic
½ teaspoon salt
½ teaspoon freshly ground black pepper

TERIYAKI MARINADE

½ cup vegetable oil
½ cup red wine vinegar
¼ cup teriyaki sauce
2 tablespoons Worcestershire sauce
1 clove garlic, minced
2 teaspoons dry mustard
½ teaspoon freshly ground black pepper
Dash of red pepper
Dash of hot sauce

Score flank steak in diamond pattern across grain on one side. Place steak in plastic zip bag. Mix marinade, pour over steak and refrigerate overnight. You wish to reserve ¼ cup marinade for basting. Remove steak from marinade and grill. Do not overcook as steak will become tough. Slice steak very thinly at an angle across grain.

Yields: 6 to 8 servings

Sweet-N-Spicy Barbequed Brisket

5	pound beef brisket, trimmed	2	cups chunky salsa
	Salt and pepper	½	cup brown sugar
1	tablespoon garlic powder	½	cup Worcestershire sauce

Preheat oven to 300°. Season brisket with salt, pepper, and garlic powder. Place in 9 x 13 inch baking dish. Mix salsa, brown sugar, and Worcestershire and spread over brisket. Cover and refrigerate overnight. Bake covered 4½ to 5 hours or until tender. Slice and serve with noodles.

Yield: 10 servings

Johnny Marzetti

1	medium onion, chopped	½	(6-ounce) can black olives, sliced
½	pound mushrooms, sliced (optional)	½	teaspoon salt
1	clove garlic, minced	¼	teaspoon black pepper
3	tablespoons salad oil	½	teaspoon dried basil
1½	pounds ground beef	½	pound spaghetti
1	(26-ounce) jar spaghetti sauce	2	cups (8 ounces) grated Cheddar cheese

Preheat oven to 350°. Sauté onion, mushrooms, and garlic in salad oil. Add ground beef and cook until browned; drain off excess oil. Add spaghetti sauce, olives, salt, pepper, and basil; let mixture come to boil. Lower heat and simmer slowly about 30 minutes, stirring occasionally. Cook spaghetti according to package directions; drain well. Layer half spaghetti, sauce, and cheese in greased 9 x 13 inch casserole dish. Repeat layers. Bake for 25 to 30 minutes. Can be frozen, but do not top with cheese. Thaw and bake with generous layer of cheese.

Yield: 8 to 10 servings

Historical Note: This casserole was created by the owner of the Marzetti Restaurant in Columbus, Ohio in the 1920s, but was especially popular in the mid '50s and early '60s.

Easy Stroganoff

1-2 pounds stew beef
  Butter, margarine or oil for
  browning
1 (10¾-ounce) can cream of
  mushroom soup or golden
  mushroom soup
1 (10¾-ounce) can French onion
  soup
1 (8-ounce) carton sour cream
½ cup sherry (optional) or red
  wine
1 small can mushrooms or
  ½ pound fresh (optional)

Preheat oven to 300°. Brown beef in butter in Dutch oven. Mix remaining ingredients and add to stew meat. Bake covered for 3 hours. Serve over rice or noodles.

Yield: 6 servings

Historical Note: Beef Stroganoff was the prize-winning recipe created for a cooking competition held in the 1890s in St Petersburg, Russia. The chef who devised the recipe worked for the Russian diplomat, Count Stroganoff, a member of one of Russia's grandest noble families.

French Beef Stew

1½ pounds stew beef, cut into
  1 inch cubes
½ cup all-purpose flour, divided
2 tablespoons vegetable oil
  Salt and pepper
2 (14-ounce) cans stewed
  tomatoes
1 (14-ounce) can beef broth
4 medium carrots, cut in 1 inch
  chunks
2 medium potatoes, cut in 1 inch
  chunks
10 ounces sugar snap peas
¾ teaspoon dried thyme
½ cup Pinot Noir wine or other
  dry red wine
2 tablespoons Dijon mustard
½ cup water
  Mushrooms and onions
  (optional)

Combine meat and ¼ cup of flour in plastic zip bag, shaking to coat evenly. In 6 quart pan, brown meat in oil and season meat with salt and pepper. Add tomatoes, beef broth, carrots, potatoes, peas, thyme and wine. Bring to boil. Reduce heat, cover and simmer for 1 hour or until beef is tender. Blend in mustard. To thicken, mix remaining ¼ cup flour with water and add to stew.

Yield: 6 servings

Green Olive Meatloaf

2 pounds lean ground round
½ cup oatmeal (instant or
   regular), uncooked
1 onion, diced
16 large stuffed green olives,
   sliced

½ cup tomato juice
2 teaspoons salt
   Dash of pepper
3 onion slices
1 cup tomato juice

Preheat oven to 325°. Mix first 7 ingredients together. Mix well but lightly. Form into loaf in 9 x 13 inch baking pan. Pat together tightly, but don't crush. Top with onion slices and pour 1 cup of tomato juice over loaf. Bake for 1½ hours, basting twice with juices in pan.

Yield: 8 servings

Tamale Pie

3 large onions, chopped
2 pounds ground beef
3 (10¾-ounce) cans tomato soup
1 tablespoon salt
1 teaspoon black pepper
2 teaspoons cayenne pepper

3 garlic cloves, minced
3 tablespoons chili powder
1½ cups ripe olives, cut in half
1 (12-ounce) can whole kernel
   corn
2 (15-ounce) cans chili beans

TOPPING
½ cup all-purpose flour
1 teaspoon salt
1 teaspoon baking powder
½ teaspoon baking soda

¾ cup cornmeal
1 cup buttermilk
1 egg, beaten
2 tablespoons oil

Preheat oven to 325°. Brown onions and beef in large skillet. Add remaining ingredients and pour into two 2 quart greased casseroles and cover. Bake for 1¼ hours. For topping, combine flour, salt, baking powder and baking soda and add to cornmeal; mixing well. Add buttermilk, egg and oil. Stir well. Spread half cornmeal mixture over each casserole. Increase oven temperature to 425°. Return to oven and bake for 25 minutes longer.

Yield: 10 to 12 servings

Barbecue Burger Casserole

2	pounds ground chuck	1	(8-ounce) carton sour cream
1	medium onion, chopped	1	(8-ounce) package cream
¾	cup barbeque sauce		cheese, softened
¾	cup regular or spicy ketchup	¼	cup chopped green onions
1	tablespoon prepared mustard	3	cups hot cooked medium egg
1	teaspoon salt		noodles
1	teaspoon pepper	2½	cups shredded sharp Cheddar cheese, divided

Preheat oven to 350°. Cook ground chuck and onion in large skillet over medium heat until beef crumbles and is no longer pink. Drain and return to skillet. Add barbeque sauce, ketchup, mustard, salt and pepper to beef mixture. Bring to boil; cover, reduce heat, and simmer, stirring once, for 10 minutes. In large bowl, combine sour cream and cream cheese, stirring until smooth. Stir in green onions and hot cooked noodles. Layer half noodle mixture in greased 9 x 13 inch baking dish. Top with half beef mixture. Sprinkle with 1 cup Cheddar cheese. Top with remaining noodle mixture and remaining beef mixture. Bake, covered, 30 minutes or until thoroughly heated. Uncover and sprinkle with remaining 1½ cups Cheddar cheese; bake 5 minutes. If desired, cover and chill eight hours, or freeze up to 1 month; thaw in refrigerator overnight. Let stand at room temperature 30 minutes before baking.

Yield: 8 servings

Pot Roast Surprise

3	(3 to 4-pound) pot roast	1	(15-ounce) can whole berry
1	large onion, chopped		cranberry sauce
1	(5-ounce) jar horseradish		Salt and pepper to taste

Brown roast and onions in Dutch oven. Spread horseradish and cranberry sauce over meat. Add salt and pepper. Cover and cook on stove or in 350° oven for 3 to 3½ hours.

Yield: 6 to 8 servings

Note: Unusual ingredients but marvelous taste!

Quick and Easy Chili

1	pound lean ground chuck	1	(10-ounce) can chopped Rotel tomatoes and green chilies
1	(16-ounce) can diced tomatoes		
1	(15-ounce) can red kidney beans	1½	cups water
		1	package chili seasoning mix
		1	package dry onion soup mix

Cook ground chuck until crumbly and drain well. Add remaining ingredients and bring to boil. Reduce heat and simmer uncovered for about 10 minutes. Can be made ahead and frozen.

Yield: 9 cups

Historical Note: Chili, like Apple Pie, is American, not Mexican, and there are several versions of its origin. Some say it was invented by chuck wagon cooks who traveled along with the cowboys. Another legend is that it was an invention of the Texas prison systems because they bought cheap and tough cuts of meats. To make them more palatable, they boiled small pieces of meat with chilies and spices.

Mustard and Green Peppercorn Pork Chops

8	center-cut pork chops	1	sprig fresh thyme or ½ teaspoon dried
	Salt and pepper		
½	cup all-purpose flour	1	cup dry white wine
1	teaspoon paprika	1	cup chicken broth
2	tablespoons vegetable oil	1	tablespoon Dijon mustard
⅔	cup finely diced carrots	1	tablespoon whole green peppercorns
⅔	cup finely diced onions		
1	clove garlic, finely chopped	2	tablespoons capers
1	bay leaf	1	tablespoon finely chopped parsley

Sprinkle chops on both sides with salt and pepper to taste. Blend flour and paprika and dredge chops with mixture. Heat oil and brown chops on both sides, about 5 minutes per side. Pour off fat and sprinkle chops with carrots, onions and garlic. Add bay leaf and thyme. Add wine and chicken broth, cover. Cook over low heat for about 1 hour. Remove chops. Stir mustard into pan drippings. Bring almost to boil, but do not boil. Add peppercorns, capers, and parsley. Serve hot over chops.

Yield: 8 servings

Roasted Pork Tenderloin with Walnut Curry Stuffing and Red Currant Sauce

2	tablespoons butter or margarine	2	pork tenderloins (about ¾ pound each)
1½	cups chopped walnuts, divided	1½	teaspoons ground coriander
1	teaspoon curry powder	1	teaspoon ground cumin
4	teaspoons olive oil	1¼	teaspoons salt
1	large clove garlic	¼	teaspoon ground black pepper

SAUCE

1	(12-ounce) jar Crosse & Blackwell Red Currant Jelly	1	teaspoon apple cider vinegar
2	teaspoons sherry	½	teaspoon ground ginger
½	teaspoon hot red pepper flakes	2	tablespoons minced shallots

Preheat oven to 350°. Melt margarine in small skillet over moderate heat. Add walnuts and cook, stirring often, until lightly toasted (1 to 2 minutes). Combine half walnuts, curry powder, oil, and garlic in food processor and process until finely ground (5 to 7 seconds). Butterfly pork by cutting along length with sharp knife until it opens up like a book. Spread walnut mixture evenly down center. Bring sides of pork together to enclose mixture. Secure with string. Combine coriander, cumin, salt, and pepper and rub over pork. Arrange pork, seam side down, in 9 x 13 inch pan. Bake until internal temperature reaches 150 to 160°, about 45 minutes. Transfer pork to platter and let rest 10 minutes covering with foil, before carving. For glaze combine all ingredients in small saucepan. Bring to boil over moderate heat. Turn down to simmer and cook, stirring occasionally, for 5 minutes. Cover and keep warm. Carve pork into ½ inch slices and spoon glaze over pork. Sprinkle with reserved walnuts to serve.

Yield: 4 servings

HERBS

Herbs have played an important role in man's life for countless years -not only in flavoring food but in his politics, romance, religion, health, and superstition. Many herbs are used in meat preparation and can easily be grown in most climates. Herb gardens might contain parsley, basil, oregano, rosemary, thyme, sage, cilantro, mint and dill, to name a few.

Grilled or Roasted Pork Tenderloin

2 pork tenderloins (use with one of the following marinades)
   (about ¾ pound each)

APRICOT MARINADE

¼ cup soy sauce

¼ cup olive oil

¼ cup sherry

1 jar apricot preserves

1 teaspoon ground cumin

   Salt and pepper to taste

TANGY MARINADE

½ cup peanut oil

⅓ cup soy sauce

¼ cup red wine vinegar

3 tablespoons lemon juice

2 tablespoons Worcestershire
   sauce

1 clove garlic, crushed

1 tablespoon chopped fresh
   parsley

1 tablespoon dry mustard

1½ teaspoons pepper

Place tenderloins in plastic zip bag. Combine marinade ingredients and pour over tenderloins. Marinate for 6 to 8 hours in refrigerator. Remove tenderloins and grill on medium heat, covered, for 30 to 40 minutes, turning once. Baste when turning. Can be baked, uncovered for 40 minutes at 350°.

Yield: 4 to 6 servings

Honey Roasted Pork

1 (2 to 3 pound) boneless pork
   loin roast

¼ cup honey

2 tablespoons Dijon mustard

2 tablespoons mixed or black
   peppercorns, crushed

½ teaspoon dried thyme, crushed

½ teaspoon salt

   Garnishes: watercress, apple,
   and orange slices (optional)

Preheat oven to 325°. Place roast on lightly greased rack in shallow roasting pan. Combine honey and next 4 ingredients. Brush about half of mixture over roast. Bake for 1 hour. Brush with remaining honey mixture and bake 30 more minutes or until meat thermometer inserted into thickest portion of roast reaches 160°. Garnish, if desired.

Yield: 8 servings

Barbeque Sauce for Pork

1	cup apple cider vinegar	1	tablespoon molasses
2	cups ketchup	1	teaspoon salt
3	tablespoons packed dark brown sugar	½	teaspoon dried crushed red pepper
1	tablespoon mustard	1	teaspoon lemon juice

Combine all ingredients in pan over low heat and whisk well to dissolve sugar. Simmer 30 minutes.

Juicy Pig

3-4	pound Boston Butt		Garlic salt to taste
3	ribs celery, chopped	2	(14½-ounce) cans tomatoes
1	large onion, chopped	2	tablespoons chili powder
½	small bell pepper, chopped	½	(24-ounce) bottle ketchup
1	tablespoon butter or margarine	¼	(2-ounce) bottle Tabasco sauce
¼	(10-ounce) bottle Worcestershire sauce		Black pepper to taste

Boil meat in garlic salted water for 1 hour and discard water. Remove and trim off excess fat. Sauté celery, onion and bell pepper in butter. Add remaining ingredients and meat. Simmer, stirring occasionally, for approximately 6 hours until meat shreds. Serve on buns.

Yield: 10 to 12 servings

BARBECUE SAUCE

Each area of the South has its own characteristic barbecue sauce. In eastern North Carolina, it is vinegar-based but becomes thicker and more tomato-based farther west. South Carolina sauce is traditionally mustard-based, while Georgia boasts a spicy and sweet thin, red sauce with tomatoes, vinegar and mustard.

Grilled Maple-Glazed Baby Back Ribs

MARINADE

1 ½ cups pure maple syrup
1 ½ cups apple cider vinegar
1 cup vegetable oil

½ cup molasses
½ cup soy sauce
3 tablespoons mustard

4 racks baby back ribs, pork or beef, cracked along backbone

Combine marinade ingredients in medium bowl and blend well. Rinse ribs and pat dry with paper towels. Place in shallow glass or plastic container. Pour marinade over and turn to coat thoroughly. Cover and refrigerate at least 12 hours, turning occasionally. Preheat oven to 300°. Remove ribs from container, reserving marinade. Place ribs in large pan and bake 50 minutes. Strain marinade into medium saucepan. Bring to boil and simmer on moderate heat 1 hour or until reduced to about 2½ cups. Set aside. Brush grill rack with oil. Place ribs on grill and cover. Brush ribs frequently with reduced marinade, turning until meat is tender and glazed, about 30 minutes. Slice ribs into individual portions and serve hot.

Yield: 8 servings

Pork and Black Bean Chili

3 tablespoons olive oil
1 teaspoon minced garlic
1 medium onion, chopped
1 (15-ounce) can black beans,
   rinsed and drained

2 (14½-ounce) cans chili style
   tomatoes, diced
1 can beef broth
2 cups pork loin, cooked and
   cubed

Heat oil in 4 to 5 quart pot. Stir in minced garlic and onion; sauté until tender. Stir in beans, tomatoes, beef broth and pork. Simmer for 20 minutes. Can be frozen. Great way to use leftover pork!

Yield: 8 servings

Greek Pork Pita Pockets

4 tablespoons olive oil
4 tablespoons lemon juice
1 tablespoon mustard
2 cloves garlic, minced

1 pound boneless pork loin cut into ½ inch slices, then cut into strips
Salt and pepper, to taste
2 large pitas

CUCUMBER SAUCE
1 cup plain yogurt
1 cucumber, peeled, seeded and chopped
1 clove garlic, crushed

½ teaspoon dried dill weed or 1 teaspoon fresh, finely minced
Salt and pepper to taste
Chopped red onion for garnish

Combine olive oil, lemon juice, mustard, and garlic. Place sliced pork (pork will be easier to slice if partially frozen) in small, flat dish or casserole, sprinkle with salt and pepper. Pour marinade mixture over pork, turning to coat well. Cover and refrigerate for 1 to 8 hours. Combine all ingredients for cucumber sauce (except red onion), cover, and refrigerate till ready to use. Remove pork from marinade and stir-fry in non-stick pan over medium heat several minutes. Half two large pita loaves and open to form pocket. Fill with pork. Top with cucumber sauce. Garnish with chopped red onion, if desired.

Yield: 4 servings

PIG-PICKING

Historical Note: An invitation to a "pig-picking" is received enthusiastically by residents of the low country. This is a very casual affair, generally held out-of-doors. Some roast a whole pig and chunks of "pulled pork" are served with plenty of spicy barbecue sauce and Texas toast. (Usual accompaniments are the ubiquitous red rice or potato salad, Brunswick stew and flat green beans or coleslaw, with banana pudding as a favorite dessert.)

Ham Tetrazzini

2 cups diced ham
 (more if desired)
2 tablespoons chopped onion
1 tablespoon butter or margarine
1 (10¾-ounce) can cream of
 mushroom soup
½ (10¾-ounce) soup can of milk
1 cup (4 ounces) grated Cheddar
 cheese

1 tablespoon parsley flakes
1 tablespoon Worcestershire
 sauce
Dash of Tabasco sauce
1 (2-ounce) jar pimentos, drained
 and sliced
1 (8-ounce) package spaghetti,
 cooked and drained

Preheat oven to 350°. Sauté ham and onion in butter. Add soup, water and cheese. Simmer until cheese melts. Add parsley, Worcestershire, Tabasco, and pimentos. Pour over spaghetti in 1½ quart casserole. Bake until thoroughly heated, approximately 30 minutes.

Yield: 4 servings

Variation
Ham and Noodle Casserole

Substitute 8 ounces egg noodles and 1 (4-ounce) can sliced mushrooms for spaghetti and pimentos.

Pepper and Herb Crusted Rack of Lamb

2 lamb racks
1 tablespoon olive oil
1 garlic clove, minced
½ teaspoon coarsely ground black
 pepper
¼ teaspoon salt

½ tablespoon minced flat leaf
 parsley
½ teaspoon fresh rosemary leaves
 or ¼ teaspoon dried
¼ teaspoon fresh thyme leaves or
 ⅛ teaspoon dried

Brush lamb with oil. Combine remaining ingredients and rub onto lamb. Cover and refrigerate 2 hours. Preheat oven to 475°. Place lamb racks in shallow roasting pan, meat side down. Roast 10 minutes. Reduce heat to 375° and roast 10 minutes. Remove from oven and let stand covered 10 minutes before carving. For larger racks and meat that is more done; roast 15 minutes at 475°, 15 minutes at 375° and rest 15 minutes.

Yield: 2 to 4 servings

Minted Lamb

1	small boneless lamb shoulder, about 2 pounds	2	cloves garlic, crushed
½	cup olive oil	¼	cup honey
2	tablespoons chopped fresh thyme	¼	cup wine vinegar
		2	tablespoons chopped fresh mint

Place lamb shoulder in plastic zip bag. Combine remaining ingredients. Pour over lamb. Seal bag and refrigerate 1 to 24 hours. Grill lamb over indirect heat about 45 minutes, until meat thermometer registers 180°. Fresh mint in the marinade really penetrates the meat. This is a particularly nice spring dish.

Yield: 4 servings

Veal Scaloppine

1	pound (¼-inch thick) veal cutlets, trimmed	4	teaspoons oil
3	tablespoons all-purpose flour	½	cup Chablis or other dry white wine
½	teaspoon salt	4	tablespoons lemon juice
½	teaspoon freshly ground black pepper		Lemon twists

Place veal on waxed paper. Flatten to ⅛ inch thickness and cut into 2 inch pieces. Combine flour, salt and pepper. Dredge veal in flour mixture. Heat oil in skillet until hot and add veal, cooking 1 minute on each side or until lightly browned. Remove veal and set aside. Pour wine and lemon juice into skillet. Bring to boil. Return veal to skillet, turning to coat with sauce. Reduce heat and simmer 1 to 2 minutes or until sauce is slightly thickened and veal is thoroughly heated. Garnish with lemon twists if desired.

Yield: 4 servings

Veal Eleganté

2 tablespoons olive oil	1 clove garlic, minced
2 tablespoons butter or margarine	2 tablespoons all-purpose flour
1½ pounds veal cutlets, cut into 2 inch pieces	1 envelope onion soup mix
	2 cups water
½ pound fresh mushrooms, sliced	¼ cup dry red wine

Heat oil and butter in skillet with lid until hot. Brown veal pieces and remove from pan. Add mushrooms and garlic to pan and cook until soft. Stir flour into pan. Add soup, water and wine, stirring to mix well. Return veal to pan, cover and simmer until meat is tender (45 to 60 minutes). Serve over buttered noodles sprinkled with chopped parsley.

Yield: 6 servings

Veal Paprika

2 pounds veal cutlets	1 tablespoon paprika
Salt and pepper to taste	¼ cup dry white wine
3 tablespoons olive oil	¼ cup chicken broth
1 tablespoon butter or margarine	1 cup sour cream
2 shallots, finely chopped	

Cut veal into ¼ inch strips. Sprinkle with salt and pepper. Heat oil, add veal and cook quickly over high heat until browned. Transfer to heated serving dish or casserole. Melt butter in same pan, add shallots and sauté until tender but not browned. Stir in paprika. Add wine and cook until reduced almost completely. Add broth and gradually stir in sour cream. Combine with meat and heat, but do not let boil. Serve hot with buttered noodles.

Yield: 6 servings

Historical Note: Paprika is the dried, ground pods of a sweet red pepper native to South America. Early Spanish explorers took the seeds back to Europe where it is now grown primarily in Hungary and Spain. Pound for pound, it has a higher content of vitamin C than citrus fruit and is prized for its brilliant red color.

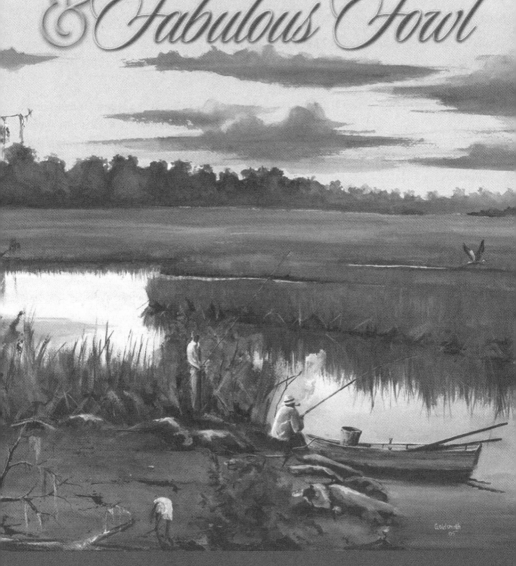

Favorites
& Fabulous Fowl

Bluff Drive: Isle of Hope's Gem

One of the most scenic streets in all of Savannah is Isle of Hope's Bluff Drive, with beautiful old estate-type homes (some dating to pre-civil war) on one side and the wide Skidaway River, dotted with private docks and numerous boats, on the other. The river is part of the Intercoastal Waterway and boats of many sizes and types pass on their way to and from Florida and northern points. Majestic live oak trees draped with Spanish Moss line both sides of the street, with arching limbs reaching out, creating a tunnel for those passing by. Bluff Drive was originally an oyster shell path used by the early inhabitants of the island.

Over the years, The Bluff has been the site of many varied and interesting events and activities. Many of the early African Americans in Savannah were baptized in the Skidaway River at the oyster shell beach just beyond the current marina. During World War II, several planes crashed in the area and survivors were rescued by local residents. Also, some of The Bluff youth were enlisted to be "plane spotters," identifying planes flying over from the shelter of an enclosed dock. Some of the original docks on the Skidaway River were double-decker, built when ladies did not swim in public. While men swam in the river, the women sat in the closely-slatted bottom story and swam in the enclosed pool underneath.

Movie studios have recognized the photographic possibilities of this special setting and a number of films have been shot here including *Cape Fear* with Robert Mitchum and *Gator* with Burt Reynolds. For the movie Glory, the street was covered with dirt to simulate the time period of the action.

There are several distinct landmarks along the drive that are worth noting. Near the northern end is a four-foot high brick structure on the river side that is controversial. Some believe it to be the only surviving beacon fire box that was used with a bonfire on top to guide returning ships home. Others contend it is a smudge pot, used to create smoke by burning Spanish Moss to repel mosquitoes and gnats. Further down The Bluff is a small concrete 8-mile pit stop marker from The Great International Savannah Automobile Races of 1908, 1910 and 1911.

Numerous legends and stories of interesting characters on The Bluff over the years abound, including pirate treasure buried under a chimney, ghosts in some of the old homes and an eccentric old lady who invited people to enter her home through the floor-to-ceiling window when her front door was broken. Bluff Drive, with all its tranquil beauty and history, is truly an Isle of Hope gem.

Chicken

Turkey

Game

Baked Chicken Breasts with Cheese Sauce

6   boneless chicken breasts, cut in half and seasoned with garlic salt, pepper, ground rosemary and thyme to taste

6-8 slices Swiss cheese

1   (10-ounce) can cream of chicken soup

1   (5-ounce) can Carnation evaporated milk

2-3 tablespoons dry Sherry or white wine

1   cup Pepperidge Farm Herb Seasoning mix, crushed

1   cup cracker crumbs (Ritz or Waverly)

4   tablespoons butter or margarine, melted

Rice or pasta of your choice

Preheat oven to 350°. Lay seasoned chicken, side by side in greased 9 x 13 inch baking dish. Cover chicken entirely with Swiss cheese slices. In medium bowl, mix soup, milk and sherry until well blended. Pour over chicken and cheese. Mix Pepperidge Farm crumbs and cracker crumbs with melted butter in medium bowl. Sprinkle over top. Cover with foil. Bake covered for 30 minutes, uncover and bake until top browns and sauce bubbles. Serve over rice or pasta. 1¼ cups sliced mushrooms may be added on top of chicken before cheese.

Yield: 6 servings

Baked Chicken Reuben

4-6 boneless chicken breasts
Salt and pepper to taste

1   (16-ounce) can sauerkraut, drained

1   (8-ounce) bottle Thousand Island dressing

4-6 slices Swiss cheese

Preheat oven to 350°. Place chicken breasts in greased casserole dish. Sprinkle salt and pepper to taste. Put 1 large spoonful sauerkraut on each chicken breast. Pour salad dressing over chicken and bake for 30 to 40 minutes, until done. Remove from oven, add slice of cheese on each breast and put back in oven long enough to melt cheese. These would also be good served as a sandwich on hot, crusty buns.

Yield: 4 to 6 servings

Bow Tie Broccoli and Chicken

2	tablespoons butter or margarine	1	cup chicken broth
4	boneless chicken breasts, cut into thin strips	½	teaspoon garlic powder
		¼	teaspoon pepper
2	cups broccoli florets	1	(3-ounce) package cream cheese, softened
1	small red bell pepper, cut into thin strips	6	ounces bow tie pasta, cooked, hot

Melt butter in large skillet over medium heat. Add chicken and cook 3 minutes or until chicken is white, stirring frequently. Remove chicken to warm plate and cover. Add broccoli, red pepper, broth, garlic powder and pepper to skillet. Cook, covered, for 5 to 7 minutes or until broccoli is tender-crisp, stirring occasionally. Stir in chicken and cook 1 minute. Remove from heat. Add cream cheese and stir until cream cheese is melted. Add pasta and toss to coat.

Yield: 4 servings

Chicken and Wild Rice Supreme

1	(6-ounce) box Uncle Ben's Long Grain and Wild Rice mix	2	(4½-ounce) cans sliced mushrooms, drained
1	cup chopped onion	6	cups diced cooked chicken (2 chickens)
⅓	cup butter or margarine	½	cup slivered almonds, toasted
½	cup all-purpose flour	½	cup diced pimiento
2	cups half-and-half	4	tablespoons chopped parsley
1	cup chicken broth	3	teaspoons salt
		½-1	teaspoon black pepper

Preheat oven to 425°. Prepare rice according to package directions. Sauté onions in butter until tender. Remove from heat. Stir in flour. Slowly stir cream and chicken broth into flour mixture. Cook and stir until thickened. Add rice, mushrooms, chicken, toasted almonds, pimiento, parsley, salt and pepper. Place in greased 9 x 13 inch baking dish. Bake for 30 minutes or until heated and lightly browned.

Yield: 6 to 8 servings

Chicken and Black Bean Enchiladas

¾ pound boneless chicken
breasts
3 slices bacon
2 cloves garlic, minced
1½ cups picante sauce
1 (16-ounce) can black beans,
undrained
1 large red bell pepper, chopped
1 teaspoon ground cumin

¼ teaspoon salt
½ cup sliced green onions
12 flour tortillas (6 or 7 inch size)
1½ cups (6 ounces) grated
Monterey Jack cheese
Shredded lettuce
Chopped tomatoes
Sour cream
Avocado slices

Preheat oven to 350°. Cut chicken into short, thin strips. Cook bacon in 10 inch skillet until crisp. Remove; drain on paper towel and crumble. Pour off all but 2 tablespoons bacon drippings. Cook and stir chicken and garlic in drippings until chicken is no longer pink. Stir in ½ cup picante sauce, beans, red pepper, cumin and salt. Simmer until thickened, 7 to 8 minutes, stirring occasionally. Stir in green onions and reserved bacon. Spoon heaping ¼ cup bean mixture down center of each tortilla; top with 1 tablespoon cheese. Roll up; place seam side down in lightly greased 9 x 13 inch baking dish. Spoon remaining 1 cup picante sauce evenly over enchiladas. Bake for 15 minutes. Top with remaining cheese; return to oven for 3 minutes. Top as desired with lettuce, tomatoes, sour cream, and avocado; serve with additional picante sauce.

Yield: 6 servings

Sun-Dried Tomato Pesto Chicken Breasts

4 tablespoons ricotta cheese
2 tablespoons sun-dried tomato
pesto

2 chicken breasts, flattened
Bread crumbs
Olive oil

Preheat oven to 375°. Mix cheese and pesto. Spread on chicken breasts and roll up tightly. Top with bread crumbs; drizzle with oil. Bake for 35 to 45 minutes or until done.

Yield: 2 servings

Chicken and Dumplings

1 (3 to 4 pound) chicken fryer or hen
1 rib celery, chopped
1 small onion, chopped
Salt and pepper to taste
Flour for thickening
¾ cup all-purpose flour
2½ teaspoons baking powder
½ teaspoon salt
1 egg
⅓ cup milk

Cover chicken with water; add celery, onion, salt and pepper. Simmer 1 hour. Remove chicken from pan; skin and debone saving broth, discard celery and onion. Return chicken to pot. In small bowl, thoroughly mix ¼ cup flour with 1 cup chicken broth and add to pot to thicken simmering on low. (Adjust thickening with amount of chicken broth.) Mix flour, baking powder, salt, egg and milk together to make dumplings. Bring chicken and broth to boil. Drop dumpling mixture by teaspoonfuls on top of chicken. Cover and cook for 15 minutes without lifting lid. Serve immediately.

Yield: 8 servings

Historical Note: A close relative of chicken and dumplings was the chicken pie of yore. This was a country dish made in the family's dishpan. The chicken was boiled until tender, dumplings were added to the pot, then more dumplings were rolled out and put on top of the pie because it was then baked. What emerged from the oven was chicken and dumplings with a blanket of golden crust.

Chicken and Dressing

1 cup (2 sticks) butter or margarine
1 whole chicken, cooked and deboned (or leftover turkey)
1 (10¾-ounce) can cream of chicken soup
1 (10¾-ounce) can cream of mushroom or cream of celery soup
1 (6-ounce) package Pepperidge Farm stuffing
2 (14-ounce) cans chicken broth

Preheat oven to 350°. Melt butter in 9 x 13 inch baking dish. Spread chicken in bottom of dish. Mix soups together and pour over chicken. Mix stuffing with chicken broth, using enough to make it soupy. Pour over chicken and stir all lightly to mix. Bake for 45 minutes to 1 hour.

Yield: 6 servings

Chicken Curry Casserole

2 whole chicken fryers or
   6 to 8 chicken breasts
2 tablespoons curry
½ rib celery
1 cup white wine
2 (6-ounce) boxes Uncle Ben's
   long grain and wild rice

1 pound fresh mushrooms, sliced
4 tablespoons (½ stick) butter or
   margarine
1 (10¾-ounce) can cream of
   mushroom soup
1 cup sour cream

Preheat oven to 350°. Cook chicken with curry, celery, wine and water to cover half way for 1 hour. Drain and save liquid. Bone chicken, remove skin and chop. Cook rice in leftover liquid according to package directions. Sauté mushrooms in butter. Combine cooked rice, chicken, soup, mushrooms and sour cream in two 2 quart greased casserole dishes. Bake covered for 45 minutes. Uncover and bake additional 15 minutes.

Yield: 8 to 10 servings

Chicken Spinach Casserole

2 (10-ounce) packages Stouffer's
   Spinach Soufflé
½ cup mayonnaise
1 (10¾-ounce) can cream of
   chicken soup
1 cup water
1 (5-ounce) can water chestnuts,
   drained and sliced

3 cups cooked and chopped
   chicken
2 cups cracker crumbs (1 sleeve-
   Ritz crackers, crushed)
¼ cup butter or margarine,
   melted

Preheat oven to 350°. Grease 9 x 13 inch baking dish. Place frozen spinach in bottom of dish and let thaw. Spread evenly after thawing. Combine mayonnaise, soup, water, water chestnuts and chicken, and pour over spinach. Mix butter and cracker crumbs and spread on top. Bake for 45 to 50 minutes.

Yield: 6 to 8 servings

Methodist ladies are known for their ability to put together a casserole at the drop of a hat, especially when there is an illness or death. Canned soup is almost always a vital ingredient and no well-stocked pantry would be without a few cans of cream of mushroom or cream of chicken soup.

Chicken Pastries

2 cups cooked and diced chicken
1 (8-ounce) package cream cheese
2 tablespoons butter or margarine
½ teaspoon salt
¼ teaspoon black pepper
3 tablespoons milk
1 tablespoon diced onion
1 tablespoon diced pimento
2 tablespoons Italian salad dressing
1 (17¼-ounce) package Pepperidge Farm frozen pastry sheets, defrosted
2 tablespoons butter or margarine, melted
Crushed croutons
Paprika

Preheat oven to 350°. In medium bowl, mix chicken, cream cheese, butter, salt, pepper, milk, onion, pimiento and salad dressing until well blended. (Soften the cream cheese and butter in microwave.) (If mixture is too dry, use little more milk and salad dressing, but do not overdo.) Roll thawed pastry sheets slightly and cut each into 4 rectangles (or you can cut into 6 for smaller servings). Place ¼ cup chicken mixture in center of each rectangle. Fold over to make triangle and crimp sides with fork. Place on ungreased baking sheet. Brush tops with melted butter, sprinkle with croutons and paprika. Bake for 25 to 30 minutes until golden brown. At end of cooking time, may brown under broiler, if necessary, taking care not to burn them. This recipe is time consuming but attractive and delicious. Freezes well.

Yield: 8 servings

Chicken Roll Ups

1 (8-ounce) can crescent rolls
3 cups cooked and chopped chicken or turkey or 2 (13-ounce) cans of chicken
1 (10¾-ounce) can cream of chicken soup
1 soup can milk
2 cups grated Cheddar cheese

Preheat oven to 350°. Separate crescent rolls. At largest end of roll, put small amount of chicken and cheese and roll to point of roll. Place rolls in 9 x 13 inch greased baking dish. Mix soup and milk together and pour over rolls. Sprinkle cheese on top. Bake about 35 to 40 minutes, or until bubbly.

Yield: 4 servings

Chicken Stroganoff

2 large boneless chicken breasts, cut in bite-size pieces
¼ cup all-purpose flour
1 teaspoon salt
½ teaspoon black pepper
2 tablespoons butter or margarine
1 medium onion, chopped
1 clove garlic, minced

1 tablespoon lemon juice
1 (6-ounce) package sliced fresh mushrooms or 2 (4-ounce) cans
1 (14-ounce) can chicken broth or more
½ (12-ounce) package egg noodles
¼ teaspoon paprika
1 cup sour cream

Shake chicken pieces in flour, salt and pepper in plastic zip bag. Brown chicken in butter; add onion, garlic, lemon juice, mushrooms and chicken broth. Simmer for 20 minutes. Add noodles and cook 10 minutes longer. Just before serving stir in sour cream and paprika.

Yield: 4 servings

Chicken Tetrazzini

1 (8-ounce) package thin spaghetti
3 tablespoons butter or margarine
1 onion, chopped
½ green pepper, chopped
1 cup sliced mushrooms
3 tablespoons all-purpose flour
1 cup milk

1 cup chicken broth
¼ cup sherry, optional
1 (8-ounce) package grated sharp cheese
6-8 green onions, finely chopped
1 (2-ounce) jar pimiento, chopped
3-4 cups cooked chicken breasts, cut into pieces

Preheat oven to 350°. Cook spaghetti 4 minutes after coming to boil; drain and place in greased 9 x 13 inch baking dish. Sauté onions and green pepper in butter. Add mushrooms. Add flour and stir until smooth. Add milk and broth; cook and stir until thick. Stir in sherry. Add half cheese and remaining ingredients to sauce and mix well. Spoon into baking dish on top of spaghetti. Top with remaining cheese. Bake for 30 minutes.

Yield: 8 servings

Historical Note: Chicken Tetrazzini is said to have been named for the Italian opera singer Luisa Tetrazzini, called "The Florentine Nightengale" in the United Sates in 1910. It was a culinary tradition to name new dishes after personalities of the day.

Chicken with Grape Tomatoes

2	teaspoons olive oil	1	clove garlic, thinly sliced
2	boneless chicken breasts (about 12 ounces)	1	pint grape tomatoes, each cut in half
¼	teaspoon coarsely ground black pepper	1	cup chicken broth
¼	teaspoon salt	1	teaspoon chopped fresh oregano leaves

In non-stick 10 inch skillet, heat 1 teaspoon oil over medium heat until hot. Add chicken; sprinkle with pepper and salt and cook 4 minutes. Turn chicken over and cook 4 minutes longer or until golden brown. Transfer chicken to plate. In same skillet, heat remaining oil over medium heat. Add garlic; cook for 30 seconds, stirring. Stir in tomatoes, broth and oregano; cook for 2 minutes. Return chicken to skillet; cook 2 minutes longer or until juices run clear when thickest part of chicken is pierced with tip of knife. Serve over pasta.

Yield: 2 servings

Chicken Worcestershire

2	boneless chicken breasts	½	cup chicken broth
2	tablespoons olive oil	1	clove garlic, minced
1	tablespoon Balsamic vinegar	½	teaspoon lemon juice
2	tablespoons Worcestershire sauce		

Split and flatten chicken breasts. Heat olive oil in sauté pan; add chicken and cook 6 minutes on each side. Add vinegar, Worcestershire, broth and garlic and simmer few minutes. Remove chicken and keep warm. Reduce sauce to desired consistency; add lemon and serve over chicken breasts.

Yield: 2 servings

Cranberry Chicken

8	boneless chicken breasts	1	(1-ounce) envelope dry onion soup mix
1	(16-ounce) can whole cranberry sauce	1	(16-ounce) bottle French dressing

Place chicken in 9 x 13 inch ungreased baking dish. Combine cranberry sauce, onion soup and dressing; mix well. Pour over chicken and marinate overnight in refrigerator. Preheat oven to 350°. Cover and bake for 1 hour; uncover and bake additional 20 minutes or until tender.

Yield: 8 servings

Easy Chicken and Rice

½	cup chopped celery	1	(10¾-ounce) can cream of chicken soup
½	cup chopped onion	1	soup can milk
½	cup chopped bell pepper	2	cups rice, cooked
½	cup diced pimiento	1	cup grated Cheddar cheese, more if desired
½	cup (1 stick) butter or margarine		Grated Parmesan cheese, optional
4	large chicken breasts, cooked and deboned		Paprika, optional

Preheat oven to 350°. Sauté celery, onion, bell pepper and pimiento in butter until tender. Combine with next 4 ingredients. Pour into greased 2 quart casserole dish. When ready to cook, top with 1 cup Cheddar grated cheese. Sprinkle with Parmesan cheese and paprika if desired. Bake for 30 minutes. Can be frozen: if freezing do not add cheese until ready to bake. Add steamed broccoli for one dish meal.

Yield: 6 to 8servings

Deluxe Chicken Pie

6   boneless chicken breasts, cut in 1 inch pieces
1   medium onion, chopped
2   tablespoons butter or margarine, melted
4   fresh mushrooms, sliced
2   large carrots, cut in 1 inch strips
1   rib celery, chopped
1   cup chicken broth
⅓   cup dry white wine
¼   teaspoon parsley flakes
¼   teaspoon chopped chives
¼   teaspoon dry mustard
⅛   teaspoon garlic powder
⅛   teaspoon chervil leaves
⅛   teaspoon white pepper
⅛   teaspoon freshly ground black pepper
1   tablespoon Worcestershire sauce
1   bay leaf
1   tablespoon plus 1 teaspoon cornstarch
2   tablespoons water
1   (10¾-ounce) can cream of mushroom soup, undiluted
½   cup sour cream
½   cup (2 ounces) grated Swiss cheese
½   cup (2 ounces) grated Cheddar cheese
2   tablespoons grated Parmesan cheese
Pastry for double-crust pie

Preheat oven to 400°. Sauté chicken and onion in butter for 5 minutes. Add mushrooms and next 13 ingredients. Cover and simmer 10 minutes; remove bay leaf. Combine cornstarch and water, stirring until blended; stir into chicken mixture, and cook until comes to boil stirring constantly. Remove from heat, and stir in soup and cheeses. Roll out half pastry and fit into 2½ quart shallow baking dish. Spoon chicken mixture into prepared pastry. Roll out remaining pastry. Cut half pastry into ½ inch strips using fluted wheel or knife. Moisten edge of pastry in baking dish. Arrange strips in lattice design over chicken filling. Make leaf cutouts (or some other design) with remaining pastry. Place on edge of pastry. Bake for 30 to 40 minutes or until lightly browned.

Yield: 6 servings

Four Ingredient Chicken

⅓	cup honey	4	boneless chicken breasts
⅓	cup Dijon mustard	1	cup ground pecans

Preheat oven to 350°. Mix honey and mustard. Dip chicken in mixture and roll in pecans. Bake for 45 minutes. Quick and easy.

Yield: 4 servings

Le Poulet et Artichoke Casserole

6	boneless chicken breasts, cut in chunks	2	(13¾-ounce) cans artichoke hearts, drained and cut lengthwise
5	garlic cloves, pressed		
	Juice 3 lemons	1	pound fresh mushrooms, thick sliced
1½	cups all-purpose flour		
1½	teaspoons paprika	½	cup chopped fresh parsley
	Salt and pepper to taste	½	cup (1 stick) unsalted butter
	Olive oil		

GRUYÈRE CHEESE SAUCE

¾	cup (1½ sticks) butter	2	cups half-and-half or cream
6	tablespoons all-purpose flour	3	cups grated Gruyère, Emmenthaller or Jarlsberg cheese
	Salt and white pepper to taste		
2	cups hot milk		

Marinate chicken pieces in 3 pressed garlic cloves and juice of 2 lemons for 1 hour in refrigerator. Preheat oven to 350°. Coat chicken pieces with mixture of flour, paprika, salt and pepper. Sauté lightly in oil. Remove chicken and place in 9 x 13 inch baking dish. Set aside. Sauté artichokes, mushrooms, parsley, juice of 1 lemon, 2 pressed garlic cloves in melted unsalted butter. Add to chicken and set aside. For sauce, make roux with melted butter, flour, salt and pepper; add hot milk, stirring quickly with wire whisk until sauce thickens. Add half-and-half and 2 cups cheese. Whisk until cheese is melted. Pour sauce over chicken and artichokes. Sprinkle with remaining 1 cup cheese. Bake for 45 to 60 minutes.

Yield: 8 to 10 servings

Hot Chicken Salad

4 cups diced cooked chicken	1 (10¾-ounce) can cream of
2 cups finely chopped celery	chicken soup
2 teaspoons onion juice	¼ cup lemon juice
½ teaspoon salt	½ cup slivered almonds
1½ cups mayonnaise	1 cup grated Cheddar cheese
	1 cup crushed potato chips

Preheat oven to 350°. Mix all ingredients except cheese and potato chips. (May be put in refrigerator overnight.) Place in greased 9 x 13 inch casserole dish and top with cheese and potato chips. Bake for 40 minutes. Serve hot.

Yield: 10 servings

Note: This is the "everyday" version of the much loved chicken salad served since 1972 at our Day On The Island Luncheon.

Lemon-Herb Grilled Chicken

½ cup olive oil	1 teaspoon salt
¾ cup lemon juice	½ teaspoon pepper
¼ cup honey	4 cloves garlic
1 tablespoon dried oregano	8 boneless chicken breasts
1 tablespoon dried rosemary	

Combine all ingredients except chicken in blender and process until smooth. Place chicken in plastic zip bag. Pour processed mixture over chicken and marinate in refrigerator at least 8 hours. Drain chicken and discard marinade. Grill chicken over hot coals until done.

Yield: 8 servings

Mexican Chicken

1	(10-ounce) can Original Rotel tomatoes		Salt, pepper and garlic powder to taste
1	(10¾-ounce) can cream of mushroom soup	10	corn tortillas
1	cup chicken broth	1½-2	pounds chicken breasts, cooked and chopped
1	large onion, chopped	1	(8-ounce) package grated sharp Cheddar cheese

Preheat oven to 350°. Combine tomatoes, soup, chicken broth, onion and seasonings in large bowl. Cut tortillas into quarters or smaller with kitchen scissors. Layer half each of tortillas, soup mixture, chicken and cheese in 9 x 13 inch baking dish. Repeat layers and bake for 30 to 40 minutes. May prepare day ahead or freeze. Thaw in refrigerator before cooking.

Yield: 8 servings

Orange-Almond Chicken

¼	cup sliced almonds	⅓	cup orange marmalade
4	boneless chicken breasts	3	tablespoons soy sauce
1	tablespoon vegetable oil	¼	teaspoon pepper
½	cup chopped shallots		Orange slices
3	ounces mushrooms, sliced		

Toast almonds in large skillet, shaking often, about 5 minutes. In same skillet, cook chicken in oil for about 5 minutes until no longer pink, turning occasionally. Remove to plate. Add shallots to skillet and cook 5 minutes until soft. Add mushrooms and cook for 5 minutes. Stir in marmalade, soy sauce and pepper. Return chicken to skillet. Reduce heat, cover and simmer for 10 minutes. Top with almonds and orange slices.

Yield: 4 servings

Mushroom Chicken Bake

4 chicken boneless breasts	1 (4-ounce) can sliced
½ cup Italian salad dressing	mushrooms, drained
¼ teaspoon pepper	⅓ cup grated Parmesan cheese
½ teaspoon paprika	

Preheat oven to 350°. Place chicken in greased 9 x 13 inch baking dish. Pour dressing over chicken; sprinkle with pepper and paprika. Bake for 30 minutes. Turn chicken over and add mushrooms; sprinkle with Parmesan cheese. Bake additional 30 minutes until tender, basting occasionally.

Yield: 4 servings

Oriental Chicken Kabobs

MARINADE

¼ cup soy sauce	¼ cup hoisin sauce
¼ cup oil	½ tablespoon hot pepper sauce
⅛ cup cider vinegar	½ teaspoon ginger
⅛ cup honey	1 garlic clove, minced
½ teaspoon black pepper	½ teaspoon black pepper

KABOBS

2 boneless chicken breasts, cut in chunks	Green pepper pieces
Small onions	Cherry tomatoes
	Mushrooms

Mix marinade and pour over pieces of chicken breast, onions, pepper pieces, tomatoes and mushrooms. Marinate for 2 hours. Thread on skewers and grill until chicken is done, approximately 20 minutes. Also good for beef or pork.

Yield: 4 to 6 servings

Note: Hoisin sauce is thick reddish brown, sweet and spicy, and widely used in Chinese cooking. Ingredients include soy sauce, peanut butter, molasses, vinegar and seasonings.

Parmesan Crusted Chicken

½ cup mayonnaise
¼ cup grated Parmesan cheese
4 boneless chicken breasts

4 teaspoons Italian seasoned dry bread crumbs

Preheat oven to 425°. Combine mayonnaise and cheese. Spread on chicken in baking dish; sprinkle with bread crumbs. Bake for 20 minutes.

Yield: 4 servings

Rotel Chicken

4-6 chicken breasts
  Water (enough to cook chicken and make 1 quart broth)
1 large onions, chopped
1 large green peppers, chopped
¼ cup (½ stick) butter or margarine
1 (16-ounce) box vermicelli
1 (10-ounce) can Rotel tomatoes

2 tablespoons Worcestershire sauce
½ pound Velveeta cheese, cut in large pieces
1 (15-ounce) can tiny English peas, drained
1 (2½-ounce) jar button mushrooms
Salt and pepper to taste

Preheat oven to350°. In Dutch oven, cook chicken in water until tender. Remove chicken and strain broth. Chop chicken. Sauté onions and peppers (do not brown) in butter or margarine. Cook vermicelli in strained broth. Add Rotel tomatoes (including juice) and Worcestershire sauce. Cook until thickened and reduced. Add Velveeta. Stir until melted. Add peas, mushrooms, chopped chicken, onions and peppers. Salt and pepper to taste. Pour into large greased casserole or 2 smaller ones. Bake for 30 minutes or until bubbly. Freezes well.

Yield: 6 to 8 servings

Historical Note: Rotel canned tomatoes have been a tradition in the southwest since the 1940s. Even a cookbook, The Snake, Rattle & Rotel Cookbook, by the legendary chuck wagon chef, Crazy Sam Higgins, was published in 1986 featuring the zesty taste of this southwestern legend. If you can find a copy, please let us know!

Poppy Seed Chicken

1 (10¾-ounce) can cream of chicken soup	3-4 chicken breasts, cooked and deboned
1 cup (8 ounces) sour cream	1 sleeve Ritz crackers, crushed
	2 tablespoons poppy seeds

Preheat oven to 350°. Mix soup, sour cream and chicken. Pour into greased 2 quart casserole dish. Sprinkle cracker crumbs on top and then poppy seeds. Bake uncovered for 30 minutes.

Yield: 4 servings

Note: This has been a favorite of our congregation for years and is often served at Family Night suppers.

Yum Yum Chicken

1½ cups chicken pieces, cooked and cut into bite sized pieces (about 3 breasts), reserve broth	¾ cup mayonnaise
	1 teaspoon curry powder
1 (6-ounce) jar Progresso marinated artichoke hearts, chopped (reserve marinade)	3 cups rice (white or combination), cooked with reserved chicken broth plus water
	½ cup grated Cheddar cheese

Preheat oven to 350°. Place chicken and artichokes in greased casserole dish. Mix reserved artichoke marinade, mayonnaise and curry powder; stir rice into mixture. Pour over chicken and artichokes. Stir lightly. Sprinkle with cheese. Bake for 20 to 30 minutes until bubbly. Serve with steamed green vegetables and fresh baked bread

Yield: 4 to 6 servings

Note: This was a member's older daughter's favorite request when she came home from college. It had no name and she named it Yum Yum.

Brined Grilled Turkey

1	gallon cranberry juice	6	cloves garlic, crushed
1	gallon apple juice	8	oranges (4 cut in ½ and
1	pound brown sugar		4 cut in ¼)
1	cup Kosher salt	1	quart water
12	bay leaves	1	fresh turkey (about 14 pounds)
20	cloves	3	aluminum roasting pans
1	tablespoon sliced fresh ginger		Wood chips of your choice, soaked

Mix half of juices with brown sugar and salt in large pot. Bring to boil for 30 seconds or so, stirring often. Set aside to cool. Prepare brine bucket (any 5 gallon non-reactive container). Put bay leaves, cloves, ginger, garlic, oranges and water in bucket. Place turkey in bucket after removing giblets and neck. Add cooled mixture and use whatever is needed from remaining juices to cover turkey completely. Cover with lid or foil and refrigerate for 1 to 2 days. Set up grill for indirect heat and use half of wood chips. Remove turkey from bucket and place in double layered roasting pans with extra foil rolled on bottom to elevate turkey. Put some of juice and all solid items from bucket into pan. Cook on medium indirect heat until parts start browning. Cover browned areas with foil. Turkey is done when meat thermometer registers 165° or when juices run clear, usually about 14 minutes per pound. Use remaining juices to baste turkey periodically. Use rest of wood chips about half way through cooking process. Cover turkey with another pan if brown enough but still needs some additional cooking. Let sit for at least 15 minutes (preferably 30 minutes) before slicing.

Yield: 8 to 10 servings

Historical Note: When the First Continental Congress met to design the Great Seal of the United States, Benjamin Franklin favored the turkey as a more fitting emblem than the eagle. To his dismay, the turkey was out-voted by a large margin. In a letter to his daughter, he wrote that the eagle was "a bird of bad moral character—and a rank coward." In contrast, the turkey is a "much more respected bird, and withal a true original native of America."

Marinated Turkey Breast

1	(5 to 7-pound) turkey breast	1	tablespoon salt
2	teaspoons chopped fresh parsley	1	tablespoon (or less) pepper
2	tablespoons oil	½	cup vinegar

Preheat oven to 300°. Place turkey breast in "Brown-In-the-Bag" in shallow baking dish. Combine other ingredients and pour over turkey breast. Close bag. Poke holes per directions and bake for 4 hours. Very good sliced cold for party and also hot with juice served as gravy as well.

Yield: 6 to 8 servings

Turkey Chili

2	pounds ground turkey	1	teaspoon red pepper
1	medium onion, chopped	2	bay leaves
1	(28-ounce) can diced tomatoes	1	tablespoon chili powder
1	(15-ounce) can tomato purée	1	teaspoon coriander
2	(15-ounce) cans red beans, drained	1	teaspoon dried oregano
1½	cups water	1	teaspoon ground cumin
3	tablespoons Worcestershire sauce	1	teaspoon dried basil
3	cloves garlic, minced	1	teaspoon leaf thyme
1	chicken bouillon cube	1	cup shredded Cheddar cheese
		½	cup sour cream

Crumble meat in large pot and brown. Add onion and cook until soft. Stir in tomatoes, purée, beans, water and spices. Bring mixture to boil; reduce heat and simmer, uncovered, stirring occasionally until thick and flavors have blended. Discard bay leaves. Serve topped with cheese and sour cream. For spicier chili, add additional spices to taste.

Yield: 8 servings

Historical Note: In North America, Indian tribes had trouble keeping wild turkeys from eating their scanty crops. Losing the battle, they decided to fence them in and feed them. Instead of pests, they became a source of protein and ornamental feathers.

Quick Turkey Chop Suey

1	pound ground turkey	½	cup chopped onion
1	(16-ounce) can bean sprouts, drained	¼	teaspoon ground ginger
1	(8-ounce) can sliced water chestnuts, drained	1	(10¾-ounce) can beef or chicken broth, divided
1	(5-ounce) jar sliced mushrooms, drained	2	tablespoons soy sauce
1	cup chopped celery	2	tablespoons cornstarch
		3	cups brown rice, cooked

In large skillet, brown turkey. Drain fat. Add vegetables, ginger and all but ¼ cup broth. Bring to boil over medium-high heat. Reduce heat, cover and simmer for 20 minutes. Combine ¼ cup reserved broth with soy sauce and cornstarch. Add to meat and vegetable mixture, stirring until thick and bubbly. Serve over rice.

Yield: 6 servings

Baked Quail or Dove Breasts

12	birds	2	cloves garlic, minced
	Salt and pepper to taste	2	teaspoons chicken bouillon granules
	All-purpose flour for dusting		
	Olive oil	1	cup water

Preheat oven to 350°. Salt and pepper birds, and dust with flour. Place small amount olive oil and 2 cloves garlic in Dutch oven and lightly brown birds. Add chicken bouillon and 1 cup water. Cover tightly and bake for 1½ hours, or until very tender.

Yield: 4 to 6 servings

Succulent Shrimp & Seafood

Barbee's Pavilion and the Diamond-Back Terrapin Farm

One of the best-known Isle of Hope landmarks was Barbee's Pavilion on Bluff Drive next to the present-day marina. Alexander M. Barbee was a veteran conductor on the horse-drawn street car between Savannah and Thunderbolt and was promoted to become the conductor on the Isle of Hope line. He was a classic entrepreneur and built the first pavilion at the end of the railroad line in 1880 for those people who wanted to have a fine place away from the city to be entertained. This pavilion burned and, in 1889, was replaced by a larger structure which soon became a popular gathering place for Savannahians, young and old. Big bands played for Saturday night dances and marathon dances, popular during the depression, were held there. Little Theater summer productions also were presented on the pavilion. Colonel Barbee also had a musical room full of unusual music boxes, where even the bed played a tune.

Years later when the railway was electrified, Savannahians rented boats at the pavilion and also ate at its restaurant. Jack Dempsey and other well-known prize fighters performed for William M Barbee, son of Col. Barbee, who had inherited his spirit. William and Rose Barbee lived above the pavilion when they were first married. In 1893, they started the Diamond-Back Terrapin Farm as an experiment and it was so successful, thousands of terrapins were shipped annually to northern markets. According to the WPA Guide to Georgia, published in 1940, the farm was on its "must-see" list at Isle of Hope: "The beautifully marked terrapins, which are not salable until they are between five and nine years old, are kept in separate pens and fed on shrimp and fiddler crabs. Thousands are kept for breeding purposes. A novelty for visitors is the terrapin, Toby, with his tricks of bowing to the ladies and playing the piano." Now, many years later, the Terrapin Farm and Barbee's Pavilion are only fond memories for the oldest citizens.

On January 19, 1909, a delegation from Savannah hosted a very special dinner at Delmonico's in New York City, hoping to secure a second round of the premier automobile races after the success of 1908. Isle of Hope played a prominent role in the menu, which included Barbee's Clear Terrapin Soup and Isle of Hope potatoes. Unfortunately, the tasty meal did not ensure success for Savannah.

Fish

Shrimp

Crab

Seafood

Pan Fried Fish

Salt and pepper
2 fish fillets
All-purpose flour
2 tablespoons olive oil
3 tablespoons butter
Juice of 1 lemon
1 tablespoon minced fresh parsley

Salt and pepper fillets then dredge in flour. Heat oil and butter in large skillet. Sauté fish 2 to 3 minutes per side (turn 1 time only and add additional butter if needed). Remove fish from pan. Add lemon juice and parsley to pan and remove from heat. Cook for 1 minute; pour over fish. Serve immediately.

Yield: 2 servings

Stuffed Flounder

½ cup chopped green pepper
1 small onion, chopped
2 ribs celery, diced
2 tablespoons oil
½ teaspoon black pepper
1 teaspoon salt

1 cup bread crumbs
1 pound crabmeat
½ cup finely cut fresh parsley
4 pounds flounder (fillets or whole)

SAUCE
½ cup (1 stick) butter or margarine, melted
½ cup water
½ cup lemon juice

Preheat oven to 300°. Sauté pepper, onion and celery in oil. Add salt, pepper, bread crumbs, crabmeat and parsley. Mix gently. Place spoonfuls of crab mixture on top fillets or cut pocket in whole flounder and stuff. Mix sauce ingredients together and pour over flounder. Bake 20 to 25 minutes or until tender.

Yield: 8 to10 servings

Broiled Flounder Dijon

3   tablespoons mayonnaise
1   teaspoon Dijon mustard
1   teaspoon horseradish

4   (4-ounce) flounder fillets
     (may use frozen)
½   teaspoon paprika
½   teaspoon dried dill weed

Combine mayonnaise, mustard, and horseradish in small mixing bowl. Spread mixture over fillets and place on foil-covered broiler pan. Sprinkle with paprika and dill weed. Broil 3 to 4 inches from flame for 10 minutes or until fillets flake easily with fork.

Yield: 4 servings

Grouper Parmesan

6   grouper fillets
1-2 ounces dry white wine or
     vermouth
½   teaspoon salt
½   teaspoon black pepper
1   cup sour cream
¼   cup fresh grated hard
     Parmesan or Locatelli cheese

1   tablespoon fresh lemon juice
¼   teaspoon lemon zest
1   tablespoon grated onion (NOT
     Vidalia as they are too mild)
Paprika
Chopped parsley
Lemon or lime slices as
     garnish, optional

Preheat oven to 350°. Place in single layer in well-greased baking dish. Sprinkle 1 or 2 ounces of wine over fish. Sprinkle salt and pepper to taste. Stir together sour cream, cheese, lemon juice, zest and onion. Spread over fish. Sprinkle with paprika. Bake for 25 to 30 minutes or until fish flakes easily when tested with fork. Garnish with chopped parsley and lemon or lime slices if desired.

Yield: 6 servings

Grouper Daufuskie

4	grouper fillets	2	tablespoons Dijon mustard
1	medium onion, thinly sliced	1	tablespoon lemon juice
½	cup mayonnaise		Paprika to taste

Preheat oven to 400°. Pat fish fillets dry and place them on greased baking sheet. Cover fillets with onion slices. Mix mayonnaise, mustard and lemon juice; stir until smooth. Spoon mixture over fish and onions. Bake for 10 minutes per inch of thickness. May be broiled, if desired. Sprinkle with paprika and serve.

Yield: 4 servings

Historical Note: Daufuskie is an island off the coast of Savannah that was first inhabited by the Yemasee Indians. There they found a type of pristine paradise, complete with an abundance of wildlife and fish, clams, oysters and shrimp.

Pecan Encrusted Salmon

⅛	teaspoon salt	¼	cup soft bread crumbs
⅛	teaspoon black pepper	¼	cup finely chopped pecans
4	(4 to 6-ounce) salmon fillets	2	teaspoons chopped fresh parsley
2	tablespoons Dijon mustard		Fresh parsley sprigs
1½	tablespoons honey		Lemon slices
2	tablespoons butter or margarine, melted		

Preheat oven to 450°. Salt and pepper fillets. Place fillets skin side down in lightly greased 13 x 9 inch pan. Combine mustard, butter and honey; brush on fillets. Combine bread crumbs, pecans and chopped parsley and spoon on top of fish. Bake for 10 minutes or until fish flakes easily with fork. Garnish with fresh parsley sprigs and lemon slices.

Yield: 4 servings

Baked Salmon

4	(4-ounce) salmon fillets	1	medium tomato, chopped or 1 (14-ounce) can diced tomatoes
2	cups chopped fresh spinach		
1	cup sliced mushrooms		
		⅓	cup Kraft Sun-Dried Tomato Vinaigrette Dressing

Preheat oven to 375°. Place salmon fillets, skin side down in 13 x 9 inch baking dish sprayed with non-stick cooking spray. Mix remaining ingredients until well blended, spoon over salmon. Bake for 20 to 25 minutes or until salmon flakes easily when tested with fork.

Yield: 4 servings

Marinated Swordfish or Halibut

½	cup olive oil	2	tablespoons lime juice
2	green onions, sliced	2	tablespoons Dijon mustard
2	tablespoons minced fresh rosemary or 2 teaspoons dried rosemary, crushed	6	(6-ounce) swordfish or halibut steaks

Combine oil, onions, rosemary, lime juice and mustard for marinade in plastic zip bag; add swordfish. Seal bag and turn to coat; refrigerate for 30 to 45 minutes. Drain and discard marinade. Coat grill racks with nonstick cooking spray before starting grill. Grill swordfish, uncovered for 5 to 7 minutes on each side or until fish flakes easily with fork. Can also broil.

Yield: 4 servings

Baked Italian Shrimp

2 pounds large fresh shrimp, peeled and deveined
¼ cup olive oil
¼ cup chopped fresh parsley
3 cloves garlic, minced
½ teaspoon dried crushed red pepper

¼ teaspoon ground black pepper
¼ cup (½ stick) butter or margarine, melted
½ cup French bread crumbs, toasted
½ cup grated Parmesan cheese

Preheat oven to 300°. Arrange shrimp in 11 x 7 inch baking dish; pour oil over shrimp. Combine parsley, garlic and peppers. Sprinkle over shrimp. Cover and bake for 15 minutes. Turn shrimp over; drizzle with butter, and sprinkle with bread crumbs and cheese. Bake uncovered, 5 to 10 more minutes.

Yield: 4 servings

Jambalaya

1 pound smoked sausage, sliced
1 cup chopped green pepper
1 cup chopped onion
½ cup chopped celery
1 garlic clove, minced
1 tablespoon all-purpose flour
1 (28-ounce) can tomatoes, undrained
2 cups water

2 tablespoons chopped parsley
1¼ cups rice
2 tablespoons Worcestershire sauce
2 teaspoons salt
½ teaspoon thyme, dried
¼ teaspoon red pepper
2 pounds shrimp, peeled and deveined

Cook sausage, green pepper, onion, celery and garlic in large pan until tender. Add flour and stir until well blended. Stir in tomatoes, water and parsley; bring to boil. Add remaining ingredients except shrimp. Return to boil. Reduce heat, cover and simmer for 20 minutes. Add shrimp; cover and simmer for 10 minutes.

Yield 12 servings

Easy Shrimp Soufflé

8	slices white bread	½	teaspoon salt
1	pound shrimp, cooked	¼	teaspoon dry mustard
2	cups milk		Black pepper to taste
3	eggs	2	cups grated Cheddar cheese

Preheat oven at 350°. Butter and cube bread. Place half of bread in buttered 2 quart casserole or soufflé dish. Put half of shrimp in casserole. Add remaining bread cubes, then rest of shrimp. Blend milk, eggs and spices in blender. Pour over casserole ingredients and cover with cheese. Bake for 40 minutes. This may be assembled ahead of time and refrigerated until cooking time.

Yield: 4 servings

Low Country Shrimp Boil

	Cayenne, cloves, garlic, bay leaves, Old Bay seasoning, black pepper and Tabasco sauce to taste	2	small onions per person (optional)
		¼-½	pound smoked sausage per person, cut in chucks
	Splash lemon juice or vinegar	1	carrot cut in quarters per person (optional)
3	small new potatoes per person	1	ear corn per person
		½	pound raw shrimp in shell per person

Boil water in large, heavy pot on stove or outdoor cooker. Season water with choice of mentioned flavorings along with little lemon juice or vinegar. Add potatoes, onions, sausage and carrots. Bring back to boil and cook until almost tender. Add corn and boil 5 minutes. Add shrimp and simmer 3 to 4 minutes more until shrimp are just cooked. Drain and dump on tables covered with newspaper. Provide cocktail sauce for shrimp. Enjoy with cornbread, slaw and watermelon.

Note: A low country favorite, this is a great feast to serve for casual affairs, even in your own kitchen or backyard. Be sure to have plenty of napkins on hand.

Kiawah Island Shrimp with Cheese Rice

½ cup chopped bacon
2 cloves garlic, chopped
⅔ cup chopped celery
1 large onion, chopped
1 medium green pepper, chopped
½ cup olive oil
1 (28-ounce) can Spanish tomatoes
2 (6-ounce) cans tomato paste

1 cup water
1½ teaspoons sugar
2 teaspoons Worcestershire sauce
½ teaspoon hot pepper sauce
Salt and pepper to taste
½ pound Polish sausage, sautéed and sliced
2½ pounds shrimp, peeled and deveined

In large skillet, cook bacon, garlic, celery, onion, pepper and olive oil until clear. Add remaining ingredients except sausage and shrimp. Simmer mixture for 3 hours; 10 minutes before serving, add shrimp and sausage. Serve over cheese rice.

CHEESE RICE

4 cups water
2 cups rice
2 teaspoons salt

1 onion, chopped
1 cup grated Cheddar cheese

Bring water to boil. Add rice, salt and onion. Bring to boil again, cover. Reduce heat to low and cook for 20 minutes. When rice is done stir in cheese.

Yield: 8 to 10 servings

Historical Note: The name Kiawah (KEE-a-wah) is derived from the Indians who lived in the area during the 1600s, where they hunted and fished. Today the island is a world-class resort and residential area.

"Sweet Georgia Shrimp" are favored by many seafood aficionados because they have less iodine flavor than gulf shrimp and are considered by many to be the best in the world.

Salsa Shrimp with Pasta

1	tablespoon butter or margarine	8	ounce angel hair pasta, cooked
2	eggs	2	(16-ounce) jars mild, thick and chunky salsa
1	cup half-and-half		
1	cup plain yogurt	2	pounds medium shrimp (steamed, peeled, and deveined)
½	cup shredded Swiss cheese		
⅓	cup crumbled Feta cheese	1	cup shredded Monterey Jack cheese
2	teaspoons dried parsley (or 2 tablespoons fresh)		
1	teaspoon dried basil leaves		Snow peas for garnish (optional)

Preheat oven to 350°. Grease 9 x 13 inch casserole dish with butter. In large mixing bowl, combine eggs, half-and-half, yogurt, Swiss cheese, Feta cheese, parsley, and basil; mix well. Spread half pasta on bottom of dish. Cover pasta with salsa. Add half shrimp and cover with remaining pasta. Spread egg and cheese mixture over pasta and top with remaining shrimp. Sprinkle with Monterey Jack cheese. Let stand 10 minutes. Recipe can be frozen at this point or baked for 30 minutes or until bubbly. Garnish with snow peas if desired.

Yield: 10 to 12 servings

Shrimp with Roasted Red Pepper Cream

1	(12-ounce) jar roasted red peppers, drained	1	(8-ounce) package cream cheese
½	cup chicken broth	2	pounds shrimp, cooked, peeled, and deveined
3	garlic cloves, chopped	8	ounces thin spaghetti
⅛	teaspoon cayenne pepper		Basil leaves for garnish

Process red peppers, broth, garlic, cream cheese and red pepper in blender. Scrape down sides. Put into large frying pan and cook about 5 minutes over medium heat. Add shrimp and cook 3 minutes longer. Cook spaghetti per package directions. Do not add salt or oil. Serve shrimp mixture over pasta. Slice basil leaves and sprinkle over top.

Yield: 6 to 8 servings

Shrimp and Grits

1 cup regular or 5 minute grits	¼ teaspoon pepper
½ cup shredded Cheddar cheese	½ teaspoon salt
¼ cup shredded Parmesan cheese	¼ cup all-purpose flour
1 tablespoon butter or margarine	2 garlic cloves, minced
3 slices bacon	½ cup chicken broth
½ cup chopped green onions	1 tablespoon lemon juice
1 pound medium shrimp, peeled and deveined	Dash of hot pepper sauce (optional)

Cook grits according to package directions, cook for an additional 5 to 10 minutes. Add cheeses and butter, and keep warm. Cook bacon in large skillet until crisp. Remove and drain on paper towel, crumble and set aside. Sauté green onions in 1 tablespoon reserved drippings in skillet for 2 minutes. Sprinkle shrimp with pepper and salt; dredge shrimp in flour. Add shrimp and garlic to skillet. Cook until shrimp are pink and lightly browned. Stir in chicken broth, lemon juice and hot sauce; cook 2 minutes longer. Stir to loosen brown bits in bottom of skillet. Serve shrimp over hot grits and top with crumbled bacon.

Yield: 4 servings

Shrimp Scampi

¼ cup extra virgin olive oil	8 ounces angel hair pasta, cooked and drained
3 cloves garlic, minced	
¼ cup clam juice	1 cup heavy cream
2 pounds medium shrimp, peeled and deveined	2 tablespoons chopped fresh parsley or dill
1 cup dry white wine	¼ cup grated Parmesan cheese
1½ tablespoons lemon juice	

In large skillet, heat olive oil and sauté garlic just until turns golden. Add clam juice and heat through. Add shrimp and then add wine. When shrimp turn pink, add lemon juice and whisk in cream. Toss with pasta and sprinkle with herbs and cheese.

Yield: 4 servings

Shrimp and Wild Rice Casserole

2 boxes Uncle Ben's Wild &
   Long Grain Rice
1 medium onion, chopped
1 green pepper, chopped
4 tablespoons butter or
   margarine
2 tablespoons lemon juice
1 teaspoon Worcestershire sauce
1 teaspoon dry mustard
½ teaspoon ground black pepper
2 (10.75-ounce) cans cream of
   mushroom soup
1 cup sharp Cheddar cheese
   cubes
3 pounds shrimp, cooked and
   peeled

Preheat oven to 375°. Cook rice according to package directions with seasoning package and set aside. Sauté onion and pepper in butter. In large bowl add rice, sautéed vegetables and remaining ingredients. Place in buttered 9 x 13 inch casserole and bake for 40 minutes.

Yield: 8 servings

Tivoli Shrimp Creole

4 bacon slices
2 medium onions, chopped
1 medium green pepper,
   chopped
2 stalks celery, chopped
2 cloves garlic, chopped
1 (24-ounce) can crushed
   tomatoes
¼ cup chopped fresh parsley
¼ cup chili sauce
1 teaspoon lemon juice
½ teaspoon salt
½ teaspoon hot pepper vinegar
¼ teaspoon pepper
¼ teaspoon curry powder
¼ teaspoon thyme powder
1¼ pounds raw shrimp, peeled
   and deveined
   Hot rice

Fry bacon until brown. Add onions, peppers, celery and garlic; sauté until soft. Add next 9 ingredients and cook for 20 minutes. Add raw shrimp and cook 15 minutes. Serve over hot rice.

Yield: 4 servings

Best Crab Patties

1 medium onion, chopped
1 medium green pepper, chopped
3 ribs celery, chopped
3 tablespoons olive oil, divided
1 pound crabmeat (white and claw meat)
2 eggs, beaten
4 tablespoons mayonnaise
1 tablespoon Worcestershire sauce
1 sleeve saltine crackers, crushed and divided
1 teaspoon Old Bay seasoning
Salt and pepper to taste
Dash garlic powder
1 teaspoon lemon juice

Sauté onion, pepper and celery in 1 tablespoon olive oil in covered fry pan. In medium bowl, mix crabmeat, eggs, mayonnaise, Worcestershire, half sleeve saltines, and spices. Add sautéed vegetables; gently mix together. Make patties into desired size. Use other half sleeve saltines to coat outside of patties. Using 2 tablespoons olive oil, sauté patties over medium heat. Do not crowd. Brown on both sides until crisp. Delicious with fried grits.

Yield: 4 servings or 12 small appetizers

Note: You may think these are Crab Cakes, but in Savannah they are Crab Patties!

Cobblestone Crab and Shrimp Casserole

½ cup butter or margarine
½ cup all-purpose flour
2 tablespoons chopped fresh parsley
2 cups whipping cream
1 cup dry white wine
2½ teaspoons salt
½ teaspoon black pepper
¼ teaspoon cayenne pepper
½ cup shredded Swiss cheese
2 tablespoons lemon juice
2 pounds medium shrimp, cooked, peeled and deveined
1 pound lump crabmeat

Preheat oven to 350°. Heat butter; stir in flour and cook 5 minutes. Stir in parsley and whipping cream and mix well. Stir in wine, salt, pepper and cayenne pepper, stirring constantly. Add cheese and stir. Remove from heat. Let cool. Stir in lemon juice. Layer half seafood (crab & shrimp) on bottom 3 quart baking dish sprayed with cooking spray. Put half cheese mixture over seafood; then repeat. Bake uncovered for 30 to 40 minutes until bubbly. Put under broiler to brown, if desired.

Yield: 8 to 10 servings

Crab Au Gratin

½ cup minced onion
½ cup (1 stick) butter or margarine, divided
2 tablespoons all-purpose flour
1 cup milk
¼ cup sherry
½ teaspoon salt

1 dash white pepper
1 pound crabmeat
1 cup crushed saltine crackers, divided
1 cup sharp grated Cheddar cheese, divided

Preheat oven to 350°. Sauté onions in ¼ cup butter in large, heavy skillet until golden. Reduce heat to low and slowly stir in flour. Slowly whisk in milk and continue cooking, stirring constantly, until sauce begins to thicken. Add sherry, salt, pepper, crab, half crackers and half cheese. Pour into lightly greased 1 quart baking dish. Top with remaining cracker crumbs and cheese. Dot top with pieces of remaining butter. Bake uncovered for 15 minutes or until top is golden brown.

Yield: 4 servings

Vidalia Onion Seafood Casserole

2 cups chopped Vidalia onions
1 cup chopped celery
½ cup chopped greens pepper
2 tablespoons butter or margarine
1 (10¾ ounce) can cream of celery soup
½ cup evaporated milk
1 (8-ounce) package cream cheese, room temperature

1 (2-ounce) jar chopped pimento, drained
1 cup cooked rice
1 cup crab, fresh or canned
1 cup shrimp, boiled, peeled and deveined
3 cups crushed Ritz crackers
¼ cup (½ stick) butter, melted

Preheat oven to 350°. Sauté onions, celery and green pepper in butter. Add soup, milk, cream cheese, pimentos, rice and seafood. Put in greased 7 x 11 inch baking dish. Mix cracker crumbs with melted butter and place on top of casserole. Cook for 30 to 45 minutes.

Yield: 6 to 8 servings

Crabbing is a popular and timeless form of recreation on the Georgia coast, enjoyed by both young and old. The only things needed are a piece of string, a chicken neck and a net and boiled crab will be on the table for dinner.

Day on the Island
Shrimp and Crab Au Gratin

1 pound cooked shrimp, roughly chopped	1 teaspoon salt
1 pound claw crabmeat, picked through for shells	½ teaspoon black pepper
	⅛ teaspoon cayenne pepper
½ cup butter or margarine	Juice of one lemon
½ cup all-purpose flour	½ cup dry white wine
½ cup milk	1½ cups grated sharp Cheddar cheese

Preheat oven to 350°. Mix shrimp and crab gently with hands. Melt butter over very low heat. Slowly add milk, salt, peppers and lemon juice, whisking briskly until smooth, about 2 minutes. Add wine and continue whisking. When sauce is completely smooth and about consistency of thick salad dressing, remove from heat. Very gently combine with seafood with large spoon, taking care not to break apart crab. Place in greased casserole dish and top with cheese. Bake for 25 minutes. (Can be frozen up to one year, double-wrapped and in freezer bag. Defrost in refrigerator for 24 hours.)

Yield: 4 to 6 servings

Note: This was always a best seller at the Day on the Island Frozen Gourmet Shop.

Savannah Crab Delight

1 large egg	Pinch or more Old Bay seasoning
3 tablespoons mayonnaise	Salt and pepper
1 tablespoon lemon juice	1 pound crabmeat
2 tablespoons chopped pimento	½ cup mayonnaise
2 small shallots, chopped	
½ teaspoon Worcestershire sauce	

Preheat oven to 350°. Mix first 8 ingredients and then gently mix in crabmeat. Place in small greased casserole and bake for 20 minutes. Remove from oven and spread ½ cup mayonnaise on top. Return to oven and bake 5 minutes more until lightly browned and bubbly.

Yield: 4 servings

Crab Quiche

1 (9 inch) deep dish frozen pie
 shell
½ cup mayonnaise
2 tablespoons all-purpose flour
2 eggs, beaten
½ cup milk
½ pound fresh crab, drained and
 picked for shells
2 cups grated Swiss cheese
¼ cup chopped green onion

Preheat oven to 450°. Bake pie shell for 7 minutes until light brown. Reduce oven heat to 350°. Combine mayonnaise, flour, eggs and milk. Add fresh crab, cheese and green onions. Pour into prepared shell and bake for 30 minutes.

Yield: 6 to 8 servings

Oyster Dressing Casserole

2 cups Pepperidge Farm stuffing
 mix
¼ cup (½ stick) butter or
 margarine, melted
1 teaspoon salt
¼ teaspoon black pepper
½ teaspoon dried thyme
¼ cup chicken broth
2 tablespoons minced onion
¼ cup finely diced celery
2 tablespoons chopped parsley
2 (8-ounce) containers oysters,
 drained

Preheat oven to 350°. Combine all ingredients except oysters; mix lightly. Pick over oysters and remove bits of shell. Cut in bite size pieces and add, mixing well with fork. Bake in 2 quart casserole for 45 minutes.

Yield: 6 servings

OYSTERS FOR SALE AT ISLE OF HOPE AND SAVANNAH

Historical Note: Daily Georgian, October 5, 1837: Oyster Hall at Skidaway Ferry—The subscriber, proprietor of this establishment, would respectfully inform friends and the public, that he continues to put up Pickled Oysters, in superior style, which he warrants to keep in any climate, and that for their better convenience, he has made arrangements to have at all time, during the ensuring season, a full supply on hand in the city. Messrs. Turner, Eastman & Co. will receive any applications or orders, which will be promptly attended to; also, Oysters in the shell put up in barrels, and delivered in two hours after being taken from the water.

William Bransby

Roasted Oysters

One of Savannah's favorite ways to entertain informally is an oyster roast. The preferred method of roasting is to place clean oysters in one layer on a thick piece of metal, such as tin, placed over hot coals. Cover oysters with a water-soaked croaker sack (burlap bag) and steam until they begin to pop open. Shovel oysters onto picnic tables where hungry guests are waiting with a canvas glove on one hand to hold the hot oysters and an oyster knife in the other. Oysters are usually served with cocktail sauce, melted butter, plenty of saltines and paper towels. Popular accompaniments include red rice and coleslaw.

For a small group, oysters can be roasted on the grill or in the oven. To grill: place oysters on grill over medium-high heat (350° to 400°) for 8 to 10 minutes or until shells just begin to open. To roast in the oven: place oysters on a large baking sheet or dish and cook at 500° until shells begin to open.

Historical Note: Today's prices don't match those of the California gold rush, when a sort of oyster cult developed in San Francisco and gold miners making an average daily wage of $10 to $20 readily paid $6 each for fresh East Coast oysters arriving in barrels.

Oysters get skinny from over-exertion during the mating season. This takes place in the warm months, which is why oysters are traditionally not eaten in May, June, July and August (months without an "r"). Oysters during the summer are safe to eat, but may not be as plump.

Savory Sides
& Such

Wormsloe

Wormsloe, the oldest continually owned plantation in Georgia, is one of the most outstanding historical sites on Isle of Hope. It was leased to Noble Jones, a carpenter, surveyor and constable in 1736. Twenty years later, King George gave Noble Jones a royal land grant to this land which was in a strategic location to guard the Narrows on the inland waterway. Thus, Jones played a key role in the colony's early defense against the Spanish by commanding a company of marine boatmen who patrolled the coastal waters.

Much of the soil in Wormsloe was poor, so it was difficult for crops to thrive. Noble Jones grew some cotton, rice and mulberry trees for silk and also raised cattle on his plantation.

Noble Jones remained loyal to the crown before, during and after the Revolutionary War. However, his son, Noble Wymberly Jones, was a patriot and leading Georgia statesman. He was elected to the Commons House of Assembly in 1755 and served twenty years. He was also elected to the Second Continental Congress and was a personal friend of Benjamin Franklin. In 1775, Noble Wymberly Jones and other patriots stole a large quantity of gunpowder from the British. He fled Savannah but was captured later and imprisoned with three signers of the Declaration of Independence.

After the Revolution, Noble Wymberly Jones gave up public service to practice medicine. Dr. Jones helped found the Georgia Medical Society in 1804 and served as its first president. He rarely stayed at Wormsloe after he inherited the plantation.

The original house at Wormsloe was made of tabby, a combination of oyster shells, sand and water, and deteriorated over the years. Dr Noble Jones' son, George, built a new family home in 1828 and descendents of the Jones family have lived there continuously since that time.

In 1972, Jones' descendants donated 822 acres of Wormsloe to the Nature Conservancy which transferred the property to the State of Georgia. The house built in the 1820's and sixty five acres are still owned by the family. Today, the donated part of Wormsloe is open to the public. Guests enter on the avenue of oaks, which has been called the "most beautiful avenue in America." They can wander along forest paths, visit the tabby ruins and pause at the family cemetery after viewing the artifacts and film in the museum.

Grits

Rice

Potatoes

Sweet Potatoes

Vegetables

Pasta

Fried Grits

1 cup grits	Garlic powder to taste
½ teaspoon salt	1 tablespoon butter
¼ teaspoon pepper	1 tablespoon olive oil

Cook grits according to package directions, but at least 20 minutes longer. Pour hot grits into Pyrex bowl or other heat proof container. Refrigerate overnight or until very solid. When ready to fry, remove grits from bowl and slice into thick pieces. Sprinkle with salt, pepper and dash garlic powder. Heat oil and butter in skillet and fry grits on all sides until brown. Saved leftover grits work well for this recipe. Good with eggs, crab patties or other seafood.

Yield: 4 servings

Grits 'N Greens Casserole

1 cup half-and-half	½ cup (1 stick) butter or margarine
6 cups chicken broth, divided	1½ cups grated Parmesan cheese, divided
1⅓ cups grits (quick cooking can be used)	½ teaspoon freshly ground black pepper
1 (10-ounce) package frozen chopped collard greens	¼ cup real bacon bits

Preheat oven to 350°. Combine half-and-half and 4 cups chicken broth and bring to boil. Stir in grits and cook according to package directions. Cook collards in remaining 2 cups chicken broth until tender, about ten minutes. Drain well in colander, squeezing out remaining liquid. Add butter, 1 cup Parmesan cheese and pepper to cooked grits, stirring until butter is melted. Stir in cooked greens and spoon into greased 2 quart casserole. Top with remaining Parmesan cheese and bacon bits. Dish can be served at room temperature or heated until browned on top.

Yields: 6 servings

Historical Note: Southerners love greens, especially collards and turnip greens. They are very low in calories, fat, cholesterol and sodium (except when seasoned with salt-pork, "fat-back") and high in vitamin A and iron. During the depression, greens and cornbread were standard fare for poor Southern families.

Baked Garlic Cheese Grits

4 cups water	¾ cup milk
1¼ teaspoons salt	2 teaspoons garlic powder
1 cup quick-cooking grits	½ teaspoon hot pepper sauce
1½ cups extra-sharp shredded	2 large eggs
Cheddar cheese, divided	¼ cup Parmesan cheese
1 tablespoon butter or margarine	

Preheat oven to 350°. Bring water to boil and gradually add salt and grits, stirring constantly. Cover and simmer 8 minutes or until thick, stirring frequently. Remove from heat. Add Cheddar cheese and butter, stirring until cheese melts. Combine milk, garlic powder, hot pepper sauce and eggs, stirring with whisk. Add grits, mixing well. Pour into 8 inch square or 7 x 11 inch greased baking dish. Sprinkle with Parmesan cheese. Bake uncovered 45 minutes. Let grits stand for 10 minutes before serving.

Yield: 8 servings

Variation
Sausage, Grits and Cheese Casserole

Add ½ pound bulk sausage that has been cooked, crumbled and drained for a Breakfast or Brunch dish.

Yield: 8 servings

GRITS

Hominy grits, or just plain grits, are an institution in the South. Hominy is made from corn that is dried on the cob then removed and soaked, causing the hulls to soften and swell. The kernels are hulled, degermed and dried again. Grits, coarse whitish grains, are ground from hominy.

SOUL FOOD

The term "soul food" referred to food made with feeling and care that came from one's soul and memory. Recipes were handed down through the generations by word of mouth. When millions of African Americans migrated to northern industrial cities, soul food became a way to recognize and celebrate their African American identity.

Pecan Pilaf

½ cup (1 stick) butter or margarine, divided

1 cup chopped pecans

½ cup chopped onion

2 cups long-grain rice, uncooked or 1 cup rice and 1 cup vermicelli (broken into ½ inch pieces)

4 cups chicken broth or beef broth

1 teaspoon salt

¼ teaspoon thyme

⅛ teaspoon pepper

2 tablespoons chopped parsley

In large skillet, melt 3 tablespoons butter. Add pecans; sauté 10 minutes or until lightly browned. Remove pecans; cover and set aside. In same skillet melt remaining butter; add onion; sauté until tender. Add rice; stir to thoroughly coat grains. Add broth, salt, thyme and pepper. Cover, simmer 18 minutes or until rice is tender and all liquid is absorbed. Remove from heat; stir in nuts and parsley.

Yield: 8 to 10 servings

Savannah Red Rice

¼ pound bacon

1 medium onion, chopped

½ green pepper, chopped

3 ribs celery, chopped

2 cloves garlic, minced

2 cups rice, uncooked

2 (16-ounce) cans crushed tomatoes

2 tablespoons tomato paste

2 teaspoons salt

¼ teaspoon black pepper

Tabasco sauce to taste

Preheat oven to 350°. Sauté bacon until crisp; remove from pan. Crumble and reserve. Sauté onion, pepper, celery and garlic in bacon fat. Add other ingredients, including bacon, and cook on top of stove for 10 minutes. Pour into greased casserole dish, cover and bake for 1 hour.

Yield: 8 servings

RICE

Historical Note: Savannahians have been compared to the Chinese because they worship their ancestors and eat a lot of rice. Rice, Georgia's first staple crop, was the most important commercial agricultural commodity in the low country. (It was labor intensive and required large numbers of slaves for construction of canals and ditches to maintain adequate supplies of water.)

Easy Brown Rice

1 cup uncooked rice
1 (10½-ounce) can French onion soup
1 (10½-ounce) can beef broth
1 (6-ounce) can sliced mushrooms, undrained
½ cup (1 stick) butter or margarine, melted

Preheat oven to 350°. Combine all ingredients in 1½ quart casserole dish; cover. Bake for 30 minutes. Uncover and continue baking 30 minutes longer. Rice should be moist.

Yield: 8 servings

Crisp Rosemary Potatoes

2 pounds red potatoes, cut into ¼ inch thick slices
1 tablespoon olive oil
2 tablespoons chopped fresh rosemary

Preheat oven to 450°. Generously oil 2 large baking sheets. Arrange potatoes in 1 layer on sheets. Brush tops with oil and sprinkle with rosemary. Roast potatoes until golden brown and edges crisp, about 20 minutes, switching position of sheets halfway. Sweet potatoes can be sliced and roasted this way.

Yield: 4 servings

Garlic Parmesan Mashed Potatoes

4 medium potatoes, baked or boiled until tender, divided
3 cloves minced garlic
1 tablespoon butter or margarine
⅓ cup sour cream
⅓ cup heavy whipping cream or half-and-half
¼ cup grated Parmesan cheese
1 teaspoon salt
¼ teaspoon black pepper

Peel half skin off potatoes and mash them with electric mixer. In large saucepan over medium heat, sauté garlic in butter for 5 minutes. Add potatoes and remaining ingredients and cook over low heat, stirring often, until hot throughout.

Yield: 6 to 8 servings

Refrigerator Mashed Potatoes

5 pounds potatoes or
    1 (22-ounce) package frozen
    mashed potatoes
2 (3-ounce) packages cream
    cheese, softened
1 cup sour cream
2 teaspoons onion salt
1 teaspoon salt
¼ teaspoon pepper
2 tablespoons butter
4 slices cooked bacon, crumbled
    (optional)
¼ cup chopped green onions
    (optional)
½ cup grated Cheddar cheese
    (optional for topping)

Preheat oven to 350°. Cook potatoes until tender and mash (or use equivalent frozen mashed potatoes.) Add next 5 ingredients. Place in greased 13 x 9 inch dish. Dot top with butter; and sprinkle top with bacon, onions and Cheddar cheese. Bake for 30 minutes. Can be made ahead of time and placed in refrigerator (keeps for two weeks). Just remove when needed and bake.

Yield: 6 to 8 servings

Scalloped Potatoes

3 cups potatoes, peeled and
    thinly sliced
2 medium-sized onions, thinly
    sliced
2 tablespoons flour
6 tablespoons butter
1½ teaspoons salt
¼ teaspoon paprika (optional)
1¼ cups milk or cream

Preheat oven to 350°. Grease 10 inch baking dish. Layer potatoes with onions and sprinkle layers with flour; dot with butter and season with salt and paprika. Heat milk and pour over all. Bake for 1½ hours. Can be covered for first 30 minutes.

Yield: 4 servings

POTATOES FOR SALE

ON THE ISLE OF HOPE: 25¢ A BUSHEL

Georgia Gazette, **December 31, 1795: Three or Four Hundred Bushels of SOUND POTATOES are available at a quarter dollar per bushel from James Parker, to be delivered on the Isle of Hope.**

Senator Russell's Sweet Potato Soufflé

4	cups (2 cans) sweet potatoes, mashed
3	eggs

1	cup sugar
½	cup (1 stick) butter, softened
1	teaspoon vanilla

Topping

1	cup brown sugar
½	cup flour

1	cup chopped pecans
½	cup (1 stick) butter, melted

Preheat oven to 350°. Mix first 5 ingredients and put in greased casserole. Mix topping ingredients and place over potatoes. Bake for 30 minutes or longer until brown and bubbly.

Yield: 6 to 8 servings

Smashed Sweet Potatoes

4	pounds sweet potatoes (about 6 large)
½	cup orange juice
½	cup heavy cream
4	tablespoons (½ stick) unsalted butter, melted

¼	cup light brown sugar
1	teaspoon ground nutmeg
½	teaspoon ground cinnamon
1	teaspoon kosher salt
½	teaspoon freshly ground black pepper

Preheat oven to 375°. Scrub potatoes, prick several times with fork, and bake for 1 hour or until very soft when pierced. Remove from oven and scoop out when cool enough to handle. With electric mixer, beat sweet potatoes with remaining ingredients until combined, but not completely smooth. Transfer to 2 quart greased baking dish. Bake for 20 to 30 minutes, until heated through.

Yield: 8 servings

Historical Note: What we call yams are really just a variety of sweet potato. Yams are a completely different tuber native to Africa, starchy, not very sweet and can grow up to 100 pounds. In his first voyage to the West Indies, Columbus discovered many new foods which he brought back to Spain, sweet potatoes being among the ship's treasures.

Sweet Potato Surprise

1 pound sweet potatoes, peeled
   and cut in half lengthwise

1¼ cups brown sugar

¼ teaspoon salt

1½ teaspoons cornstarch

⅛ teaspoon cinnamon

1 teaspoon shredded orange peel

1 (15.25-ounce) can apricot
   halves, drained with liquid
   reserved or 1 (20-ounce) can
   crushed pineapple, drained
   with liquid reserved

2 tablespoons butter

½ cup pecan halves

Preheat oven to 375°. Place potatoes in greased 6 x 10 inch baking dish. Combine sugar, salt, cornstarch, cinnamon and orange peel with 1 cup syrup from apricots or pineapple. Cook and stir until boiling. Boil for 2 minutes; add apricots, butter and pecan halves. Pour over potatoes and bake for 45 minutes.

Yield: 6 to 8 servings

Parmesan Roasted Asparagus

2½ pounds fresh asparagus
   (about 30 large)

2 tablespoons olive oil

½ teaspoon kosher salt

¼ teaspoon freshly ground black
   pepper

½ cup freshly grated Parmesan
   cheese

2 lemons cut in wedges for
   serving

Preheat oven to 400°. If asparagus stalks are thick, peel bottom half of each. Lay in single layer on sheet pan covered with foil and drizzle with olive oil. Sprinkle with salt and pepper. Roast for 15 to 20 minutes until tender. Sprinkle with Parmesan and return to oven for another minute. Serve with lemon wedges. Use thick asparagus to avoid over cooking.

Yield: 6 servings

Note: Feta or blue cheese may be substituted for Parmesan cheese. 2 tablespoons of balsamic vinegar may be drizzled over asparagus before roasting and omit cheese.

Bean Bundles

2 (14½-ounce) cans whole green beans, good quality

4 slices bacon

1 cup Catalina dressing

Preheat oven to 300°. Microwave bacon until about half done and slice each piece lengthwise. Wrap about 8 long beans with narrow strip of bacon and place bundles in 9 x 13 inch baking dish. Cover with Catalina dressing and marinate overnight. Cook in oven until warm, about 20 minutes. These make an attractive and delicious addition to a luncheon plate.

Yield: 8 servings

Broccoli and Cauliflower Gratin

2 pounds fresh broccoli and/or cauliflower flowerets, rinsed

1½ cups mayonnaise

1 cup (4 ounces) shredded Cheddar cheese

1 (3-ounce) package shredded Parmesan cheese

4 green onions or 1 small yellow onion, sliced

2 tablespoons Dijon mustard

¼ teaspoon ground red pepper

3 tablespoons Italian-seasoned bread crumbs

Preheat oven to 350°. Arrange flowerets in 2 quart baking dish, coated with non-stick spray. Cover with plastic wrap, vent, and microwave on high for 3 to 4 minutes, until crisp-tender. Pour off any liquid. Stir together mayonnaise and next 5 ingredients. Spoon over flowerets. Sprinkle with bread crumbs. Bake 20 to 25 minutes.

Yield: 8 servings

Broccoli Casserole

2 (10-ounce) packages frozen broccoli

1 (10¾-ounce) can cream of mushroom soup

2 eggs, lightly beaten

½ cup mayonnaise

1 tablespoon grated onion

1 cup grated cheese

½ sleeve Ritz crackers, crushed

Preheat oven to 400°. Cook frozen broccoli in salted, boiling water for 5 minutes; drain. Combine broccoli with next 5 ingredients in buttered 1½ quart casserole. Top with crackers. Bake for 20 to 30 minutes or until bubbly.

Yield: 6 to 8 servings

Cabbage Casserole

1	small cabbage, chopped	1	(10¾-ounce) can cream of
1	small onion, thinly sliced		mushroom soup
	Salt and pepper to taste	¼	cup mayonnaise
4	tablespoons (½ stick) butter, melted		

TOPPING

1	sleeve Ritz crackers, crushed	1	cup (4-ounces) shredded
4	tablespoons (½ stick) butter or margarine, melted		Cheddar cheese

Preheat oven to 350°. Place cabbage in 9 x 13 inch greased casserole. Layer onion on top. Salt and pepper to taste and cover with melted butter. Mix soup and mayonnaise together and pour over all. For topping; mix Ritz crackers, butter and cheese. Place on top of casserole. Bake uncovered for 45 minutes.

Yield: 8 to 10 servings

Eggplant Parmigiana

2	medium eggplants	2	teaspoons dried oregano (optional)
3	eggs, beaten		
1½	cups dried bread crumbs	1	(8-ounce) package sliced mozzarella cheese, divided
¾	cup olive oil		
½	cup grated Parmesan cheese (or more if needed)	3	(8-ounce) cans tomato sauce

Preheat oven 350°. Peel eggplant; cut into ¼ inch thick slices. Dip each slice into beaten eggs, then into crumbs. Sauté in hot olive oil until golden brown on both sides. Place layer eggplant in 9 x 13 inch baking dish; sprinkle with Parmesan cheese and oregano. Repeat layers until all eggplant is used. Top with mozzarella cheese and tomato sauce. Bake uncovered for 30 minutes or until sauce is bubbly and cheese is melted.

Yield: 4 to 6 servings

Glazed Carrots

1½ pounds carrots, peeled and sliced
1 cup chicken broth or orange juice
3 tablespoons brown sugar
Pinch of pepper
6 tablespoons butter
Chopped parsley
Salt and pepper

Boil carrots slowly in covered saucepan with broth, sugar, pepper and butter until carrots are tender and liquid has reduced to syrupy glaze, about 30 to 40 minutes. Correct seasoning if needed. Sprinkle with parsley. Add prepared mustard to seasoning for an extra zip.

Yield: 6 servings

Corn Pudding

2 eggs, beaten
2 tablespoons sugar
1¼ cups milk
4 tablespoons all-purpose flour
½ teaspoon salt
3 tablespoons butter or margarine, melted
2 (14¾-ounce) cans creamed corn

Preheat oven to 375°. Beat eggs, sugar, milk, flour, salt, and butter together; stir in corn. Bake in 9 x 13 inch greased casserole dish for 10 to 15 minutes; stir. Bake 5 to 10 minutes more; stir again. Move to top rack. Bake until knife inserted in center comes out clean and top is slightly brown, approximately 30 minutes longer.

Yield: 8 to 10 servings

Grilled Portobella Mushrooms

6 portobella mushrooms
5 garlic cloves, minced
½ cup balsamic vinegar
2 teaspoons olive oil
1 teaspoon fresh basil, chopped
1 teaspoon fresh chopped parsley
Salt and pepper to taste

Discard portable stems and wipe mushrooms clean using wet paper towel. Whisk garlic with vinegar, oil, herbs, salt and pepper. Marinate mushrooms in mixture for 1 hour. Preheat grill. Grill mushrooms on an oiled rack or basket for 3 to 4 minutes per side.

Yield: 6 servings

Okra Casserole

3	cups okra, sliced	¾	teaspoon salt
1	(10-ounce) can diced tomatoes and green chilies undrained	⅛	teaspoon pepper
		¼	cup vegetable oil
1	medium onion, chopped	¾	cup crushed potato chips
1	medium green pepper, chopped	¼	cup bread crumbs

Preheat oven to 400°. Place okra in lightly greased 2 quart baking dish. Mix tomatoes, onion and bell pepper; pour over okra. Sprinkle with salt and pepper. Pour oil over mixture. Cover loosely with aluminum foil and bake 1 hour; stirring occasionally. Mix potato chips and bread crumbs. Sprinkle over casserole and bake an additional 15 minutes uncovered. Good served over rice.

Yield: 8 servings

Historical Note: Okra (often referred to as Gumbo), thought to be of African origin, was brought to the United States three centuries ago by African slaves. Grown in tropical climates, it is in the same family as hibiscus and cotton.

AFRICAN INFLUENCE

Historical Note: Both the food and style of cooking in the South were influenced by the African slaves. Not only did the slaves introduce new foods such as okra, yams, black-eyed peas, collard greens, sesame seeds and watermelon, but they also brought cooking techniques such as deep-fat frying. Southern food replaced the plain, bland English cooking and African Americans developed much of what is now thought of as Southern cooking.

Soy Sauce Onion

1	large Vidalia onion	1	tablespoon soy sauce
1	tablespoon butter		

Peel onion. Slice down as if quartering onions, but do not cut all the way through. In center of onion, place pat of butter. Place in shallow dish and pour soy sauce over onion. Cover dish with wax paper and microwave for 8 minutes. Delicious with beef or chicken!

Yield: 2 servings

Vidalia Onion Casserole

6-7 Vidalia onions, peeled and sliced

½-¾ cup grated Parmesan cheese

⅓ cup butter or margarine

1 cup crushed Ritz crackers, divided

Preheat oven to 325°. Sauté onions in butter until still crunchy. Place half onions in greased 2 quart casserole. Sprinkle with half cheese and half crackers. Repeat. Bake for 30 minutes.

Yield: 6 servings

Note: The Georgia state vegetable is the Vidalia onion which now has an international reputation as the world's sweetest onion. The sugar content is comparable to that of an apple, it is low in calories and said to be an aid to digestion.

Note: Vidalia onions are full of moisture and will go bad quickly if allowed to touch each other. They can be wrapped in foil or paper towels and stored in the refrigerator or stored on a rack in a cool area such as the garage. Many Savannahians store them in pantyhose with a knot tied between each onion. Hang in a cool, dry, well-ventilated area and cut below the knot when you need one.

Sprite Fried Onion Rings

Vidalia onions

Self-rising flour

Can of Sprite

Vegetable oil

Peel onions and cut in rings. Mix Sprite with flour until loose batter consistency. Dip onions in batter and fry in vegetable oil (approximately 375°). Drain on paper towels. So sweet and so good!

Ratatouille

½	pound eggplant, peeled and cut in 1½ x ½ x ¼ inch slices	1-1½	pounds tomatoes, seeded and chopped or 1 (14-ounce) can chopped tomatoes
3	teaspoons salt	1	(8-ounce) package mushrooms, sliced
3	tablespoons olive oil		
½	onion, chopped	¼	teaspoon black pepper
2	medium green peppers, chopped	2	teaspoons dried basil

Mix eggplant and zucchini with 1 teaspoon salt and allow to stand for 30 minutes. Drain and blot dry. Sauté with 2 tablespoons olive oil until lightly browned. Remove from pan. In same skillet, cook onions, peppers, mushrooms and garlic in 1 tablespoon olive oil. Add eggplant and zucchini and tomatoes, season with 2 teaspoons salt, pepper and basil. Cook covered for 20 minutes. Uncover and continue cooking for 10 minutes.

Yield: 6 to 8 servings

Spinach Casserole

3	(10-ounce) packages frozen chopped spinach	4	tablespoons butter, melted
1	cup sour cream	½	cup bread crumbs
1	envelope Lipton Onion Soup mix	¼	cup grated Parmesan cheese

Preheat oven to 325°. Cook spinach 5 minutes and drain. Mix 1 cup sour cream with onion soup and drained spinach; put in 1½ quart greased casserole dish. Mix butter, bread crumbs and Parmesan cheese. Place on top of spinach mixture. Bake for 30 to 40 minutes.

Yield: 8 to 10 servings

Church Homecoming Squash Casserole

2-3 pounds yellow squash, sliced
3 tablespoons chopped onion
½ cup (1 stick) butter, melted and divided
2 eggs, beaten

1¼ cups Ritz cracker crumbs, (divided)
½ cup milk
1 cup (4 ounces) grated Cheddar cheese, divided
Salt and pepper, to taste

Preheat oven to 350°. Cook squash and onions in small amount of water until tender. Drain and mash; add ¼ cup butter and eggs; mix. Stir in 1 cup cracker crumbs and milk. Add half cheese, salt and pepper. Pour into 1½ quart greased casserole. Top with remaining ¼ cup melted butter, remaining cheese and cracker crumbs mixed together. Bake for 1 hour or until brown.

Yield: 6 servings

Variation
Sour Cream Squash Casserole

Omit milk and add 1 cup sour cream, 1 (10¾-ounce) can cream of chicken soup and additional shredded cheese.

Note: This was always a requested recipe at the annual Homecoming Sunday luncheon.

Squash Dressing

2 cups cooked squash
2 cups finely crumbled cornbread
2 eggs, beaten
1 large onion, chopped
½ cup chopped celery

1 (10¾-ounce) can cream of chicken soup
½ cup butter, melted
Pepper to taste
Rubbed sage to taste (approximately ½ teaspoon)

Preheat oven to 325°. Drain cooked squash thoroughly and mash. Add other ingredients and stir. Put in buttered 9 inch casserole and bake for 45 minutes.

Yield: 8 servings

Butternut Squash Casserole

1	large butternut squash	¾	cup sugar
3	large eggs, beaten	½	teaspoon ground ginger
⅓	cup butter or margarine, melted	½	teaspoon coconut flavoring or 2 tablespoons flaked coconut
½	cup milk		

Preheat oven to 350°. Cut butternut squash in half lengthwise. Place squash cut side down in casserole dish (appropriate in size to squash) sprayed with non-stick spray. Bake for 40 minutes. Scoop out and mash cooked butternut squash. Combine 2 cups squash with remaining ingredients. Place in 1½ quart casserole dish lightly sprayed with nonstick spray. Bake for 1 hour or until firm in center. Both coconut flavoring and flaked coconut can be used or ½ teaspoon vanilla flavoring can be substituted.

Yield: 6 to 8 servings

Oven Roasted or Grilled Vegetables

1	medium zucchini, cut in bite size pieces	1	red onion, quartered
1	medium summer squash, cut in bite size pieces		Mushrooms, eggplant, broccoli, etc. (optional)
1	medium red bell pepper, cut in bite size pieces	3	tablespoons extra-virgin olive oil
1	medium yellow bell pepper, cut in bite size pieces	1	teaspoon salt
1	pound fresh asparagus, cut in bite size pieces	½	teaspoon freshly ground black pepper

Preheat oven to 450°. Toss all vegetables with olive oil, salt, and pepper to mix and coat. (Using large zip bag makes this process easy.) Refrigerate if using later in the day. When ready to cook, spread out evenly in large roasting pan. Roast for 30 minutes; stir occasionally until vegetables are lightly browned and tender.

When grilling use grill vegetable basket and cook vegetables uncovered until tender and slightly charred, turning occasionally.

Yield: 6 to 8 servings

Michie Tavern Stewed Tomatoes

4 cups peeled and quartered whole tomatoes	2 tablespoons butter or margarine, melted
¼ cup sugar	½ teaspoon salt
	6 biscuits, baked

Mix first 4 ingredients in medium size saucepan. Crumble baked biscuits over tomatoes. Cover and cook for 15 minutes.

Yield: 6 to 8 servings

Tomato Pie

1 deep dish pie shell	½ cup mayonnaise
1 tablespoon Dijon mustard	3 tablespoons shredded fresh basil
¾ cup (3 ounces) shredded yellow Cheddar cheese	2-3 large tomatoes, peeled and sliced
¾ cup (3 ounces) shredded white Cheddar cheese	½ cup grated Parmesan cheese
½ cup chopped green onions	

Preheat oven to 350°. Bake shell for 8 minutes. Spread mustard on bottom of baked pie shell. Mix Cheddar cheeses, green onions, mayonnaise and basil. Layer half tomatoes, half cheese mixture, remaining tomatoes and cheese mixture. Sprinkle Parmesan cheese on top. Bake for 45 minutes. Spinach leaves, bacon, or ham may be added.

Yield: 8 servings

Sweet and Sour Green Beans

2 (15.5-ounce) cans French green beans	½ cup slivered almonds
1 small red onion, sliced in rings	6 tablespoons sugar
8 slices bacon	6 tablespoons raspberry vinegar

Preheat oven to 350°. Place green beans in greased 1½ quart casserole dish and place onion rings over beans. Fry bacon, reserving drippings in pan. Quarter bacon strips, place over onions and sprinkle with almonds. Add sugar and vinegar to bacon drippings and heat. Pour over casserole and refrigerate several hours or overnight. Bake 40 to 45 minutes.

Yield: 8 servings

Roasted Vegetable Marinara

1   each red and yellow bell
    pepper, cut in strips or large
    chunks
1   large onion, diced
1   large portobella mushroom,
    diced
1   large carrot, diced
½   teaspoon salt and pepper

¼   cup olive oil
3   tablespoons chopped garlic
½   (26-ounce) jar marinara sauce
¼   cup each fresh shredded basil,
    oregano and thyme
1   pound penne pasta or bowtie
    pasta), cooked
1   cup grated Parmesan cheese

Preheat oven 425°. Combine first 4 ingredients. Toss with salt, pepper and olive oil in large plastic zip bag. Spread on baking sheet and roast about 20 minutes. Remove from oven. In large saucepan sauté garlic with roasted vegetables for about 2 minutes; add marinara sauce. Cook an additional 2 minutes. Add fresh herbs and cook for 1 minute. Toss with cooked pasta. Top with grated Parmesan cheese. Additional marinara sauce may be added.

Yield: 4 to 6 servings

Easy Old-Fashioned Macaroni and Cheese

¼   cup butter or margarine
¼   cup all-purpose flour
1   teaspoon salt
2   cups milk

2   cups (8 ounces) shredded
    Cheddar cheese
1   (7 or 8-ounce) package elbow
    macaroni, cooked and
    drained

Preheat oven to 350°. In large glass measuring cup or microwave-safe bowl, melt butter in microwave. Stir in flour and salt and mix well. Add milk, stirring well. Microwave about 3 minutes on high. Remove and stir well to eliminate lumps. Return to microwave and cook on high until mixture thickens (about 3 to 4 minutes). Remove and stir in cheese a little at a time to melt. Layer half macaroni and cheese sauce in casserole dish; repeat layers. Bake 20 to 25 minutes.

Yield: 8 servings

Cookies, Cakes & Confections

Isle of Hope's Resident Ghosts

Like most other historic areas of Savannah, Isle of Hope can claim a friendly ghost or two in at least one of the older homes built shortly after the Civil War. The current residents moved into this house in 1958, and about eight years later their maid said she had seen an old woman upstairs. The resident laughed and thought she perhaps had an overactive imagination. On several other occasions, the maid reported that "the old woman stepped in front of her, was brushing her hair in the daughter's bedroom" and that she had seen both an old man and old woman upstairs.

Some time later, the residents' two sons reported hearing a strange noise upstairs after going to bed that sounded like "Cush-cush," and this became a nickname for the unseen resident. Finally, one night when the owners were home alone, sitting downstairs directly under the daughter's bedroom, they heard such bumping and thumping, they could not ignore. When they checked upstairs, however, they saw nothing out of the ordinary.

Miss Mamie Jackson and her bachelor brother lived in the house for many years prior to the current residents. She was quite a character and terrified the children in the neighborhood by screaming at them from her upstairs porch anytime they ventured onto her property.

While the only person who ever saw the old woman and man was the maid, there were enough unexplainable noises to make one wonder. Over the years, the noises have gradually faded away. Perhaps Miss Mamie has decided her home is in good hands and she has moved on, or she has become so comfortable with the family, she no longer needs to make her presence known.

Cookies and Bars

Cakes

Pies

Miscellaneous Desserts

Boterkoek (Dutch Shortbread)

1 cup butter or margarine,
   softened
1 cup sugar

1 egg
2 cups all-purpose flour

Preheat oven to 350°. Grease and flour 8 inch round baking pan. Cream butter and sugar. Add egg and flour. Place in pan, spread evenly and smooth top of mix with wet hand. Bake for 35 to 40 minutes until golden brown.

Yield: 12 to 16 thin slices

"Oh My Gosh" Stuffed Brownies

1 (19-ounce) box Brownies with
   Walnuts mix

3 large Symphony Bars with
   Almonds & Toffee

Preheat oven to 350°. Prepare brownies according to mix, using 3 egg method. Spray 9 x 13 inch pan with non-stick cooking spray. Put half brownie mix in pan. Place 3 Symphony bars across dough and cover completely with remaining mix. Bake for 21 to 24 minutes. Cool completely and cut into squares. Very rich and freezes well.

Yield: 40 squares

Chocolate Chewies

2½ cups confectioners' sugar
⅓ cup cocoa
2 tablespoons all-purpose flour

3 egg whites
1 cup chopped pecans

Preheat oven to 350°. Line cookie sheets with parchment paper. Place sugar, cocoa and flour in mixer bowl and beat until well blended. Beat in egg whites one at a time, scraping bowl as necessary. Beat at high speed for 1 minute. Beat in pecans. Drop by tablespoonfuls onto sheets, leaving 2 inches between cookies for spreading. Bake one sheet at a time for 15 minutes on middle rack, turning sheet around halfway through baking time. Cool on paper. Place cookies on paper in freezer and freeze for 1 hour. Remove from freezer; peel paper off cookies. (Eggs separate best when cold, but egg whites need to be at room temperature for greater volume when whipped. When baking, all ingredients needs to be at room temperature for best results.)

Yield: 24 cookies

Note: This recipe is similar to the Number 1 cookie seller at Gottlieb's Bakery that we all remember. The bakery is now closed.

Brownie Cookies

½ cup (1 stick) butter or margarine

4 squares unsweetened chocolate, chopped

3 cups semi-sweet chocolate chips, divided

1½ cups all-purpose flour

½ teaspoon baking powder

½ teaspoon salt

4 eggs

1½ cups sugar

2 teaspoons vanilla

2 cups chopped pecans

Preheat oven to 350°. Combine butter, unsweetened chocolate and 1½ cups chocolate chips in large, heavy saucepan. Cook over low heat, stirring constantly until butter and chocolate melt. Cool. Combine flour, baking powder and salt; set aside. Beat eggs, sugar and vanilla at medium speed with electric mixer. Gradually add dry ingredients, beating well. Add melted chocolate mixture and stir in remaining chocolate chips and pecans. Drop by 2 tablespoonfuls 1 inch apart onto parchment paper-lined baking sheets. Bake for 10 minutes. Cool slightly on baking sheets before removing to wire racks to cool completely.

Yield: 2 dozen

Historical Note: *According to culinary historians, the first record of cookies was their use as test cakes. A small amount of batter was baked to test the oven temperature.*

Cowboy Cookies

1 cup (2 sticks) butter or margarine

1 cup sugar

1 cup brown sugar

1 teaspoon vanilla

2 eggs

2 cups all-purpose flour

1 teaspoon baking soda

½ teaspoon salt

½ teaspoon baking powder

2 cups oats, quick cooking or regular, uncooked

1 (12 ounce) package semi-sweet chocolate chips

Preheat oven to 350°. Cream butter and sugars; add vanilla. Add eggs and beat until light and fluffy. Stir in dry ingredients and blend well. Mix in oats, chocolate chips and vanilla. Drop by teaspoonfuls on greased cookie sheet and bake about 10 minutes.

Yield: 10 dozen

Variation
Cowgirl Cookies

Add 1 cup coconut and 2 cups corn flakes instead of chocolate chips.

Kourabiedes (Greek Butter Cookies)

1 pound (4 sticks) unsalted butter, softened	1 teaspoon vanilla
½ cup sugar	4 cups sifted all-purpose flour
1 egg yolk	3 cups sifted confectioners' sugar (set aside)

Preheat oven to 350°. In large mixing bowl, beat butter and sugar together until creamy. Add egg yolk and vanilla, mixing well until blended. Gradually add flour on slow speed to make soft dough. Pinch off pieces of dough and shape carefully into small crescents. Flour hands if necessary. Place on ungreased cookie sheet 1 inch apart. Bake for 20 minutes or until lightly browned. Cool slightly before removing from cookie sheet. Carefully place on prepared flat surface which has been sprinkled with confectioners' sugar. Sprinkle more confectioners' sugar over cookies. Cool.

Yield: 5 dozen

Red Raspberry Chocolate Squares

2½ cups all-purpose flour	1 egg
1 cup sugar	1 (12-ounce) jar seedless red raspberry jam
¾ cup finely chopped pecans	
1 cup (2 sticks) butter or margarine, softened	1 (12-ounce) bag semi-sweet chocolate chips

Preheat oven to 350°. Mix together flour, sugar, pecans, butter and egg. Set aside 1½ cups mixture. Press remaining mixture onto bottom of greased 9 x 13 inch baking pan; spread jam over top. (Jam can be slightly melted in microwave for easier spreading.) Sprinkle with chocolate chips. Dot remaining mixture over the top. Bake for 8 to 10 minutes. Remove from oven and swirl top to create marbled effect. Return to oven and bake 40 to 45 minutes or until lightly browned. Cool completely in pan and cut into bars.

Yield: 24 to 32 squares

Variation
Double Chocolate Raspberry Squares

Mix brownie mix according to package directions. Spread two-thirds onto bottom of greased 9 x 13 inch baking pan; dot with (8-ounce) jar raspberry jam. Sprinkle with (6-ounce) package chocolate chips. Top with remaining brownie mixture. Bake according to mix directions.

Macadamia and Coconut Bars

BOTTOM LAYER

½ cup (1 stick) unsalted butter, softened

½ cup light brown sugar

1 large egg

¼ teaspoon salt

1¼ cups all-purpose flour

TOP LAYER

1½ cups macadamia nuts, cut up

2 tablespoons all-purpose flour

½ teaspoon baking powder

2 large eggs

1 teaspoon vanilla

1 cup light brown sugar, packed

2 cups (6 ounces) shredded coconut, divided

Preheat oven to 350°. For bottom layer: beat butter until soft. Add sugar and blend until smooth. Beat in egg and salt. Add flour and mix until just incorporated. Press into bottom of aluminum foil lined 9 x 13 inch pan. Bake on middle rack until set, approximately 15 minutes. For top layer: stir all ingredients together, using only half coconut. Place mixture evenly over top of crust (very thin layer) and sprinkle with remaining coconut. Bake for 25 minutes, turning pan once during baking. Cool; peel off foil. Refrigerate and cut into bars.

Yield: 48 bars

Variation
Salted Nut Bars

BOTTOM LAYER, FOLLOW ABOVE DIRECTIONS.

TOP LAYER

2 cups mixed nuts or peanuts

1 cup butterscotch chips

½ cup light corn syrup

2 tablespoons butter or margarine

Sprinkle nuts evenly over crust. Heat remaining ingredients over low heat, stirring occasionally, just until chips are melted. Drizzle evenly over nuts. Bake for 5 minutes. Cut while warm for easier cutting.

***Historical Note:** The macadamia nut tree originated in the rain forests of Queensland, Australia, but in 1882 was taken to Hawaii where most of the world's macadamias are now grown.*

Swirled Chip Cake Mix Cookies

1	box marble or fudge swirl cake mix	½	cup oil
		1	egg
3	tablespoons plus 1 tablespoon water (divided)	½	(6 ounce) bag milk chocolate chips

Preheat oven to 350°. Mix cake mix (not including fudge packet in box) with 3 tablespoons water, oil, and egg. Transfer about quarter dough into another bowl. Stir fudge packet into remaining dough along with 1 tablespoon water and blend. Stir chocolate chips into remaining light batter. Add dark batter to original dough and swirl with knife. Drop by large tablespoons onto ungreased cookie sheet. Flatten slightly with fingers. Bake for about 15 minutes.

Yield: 2½ dozen cookies

Variations
Praline Pecan Cake Mix Cookies

1	box yellow cake mix	1	egg
4	tablespoons water	2	tablespoons brown sugar
½	cup oil	1	cup chopped pecans

Mix all ingredients together and follow previous directions.

Sugar Cake Mix Cookies

1	box yellow cake mix	1	egg
4	tablespoons water		Sugar
½	cup oil		

Follow previous directions and sprinkle with sugar.

Cinnamon Sugar Cake Mix Cookies

Follow previous directions with mixture of cinnamon and sugar.

Double Chocolate Cake Mix Cookies

1	box devils food or dark chocolate cake mix	½	cup oil
		1	egg
4	tablespoons water	1	cup chocolate chips

Follow previous directions.

My Mama's Chewy Squares

½ cup (1 stick) butter or margarine

1 pound (16-ounce) box brown sugar

3 large eggs

2 cups all-purpose flour

1 tablespoon baking powder

1 teaspoon salt

1 teaspoon vanilla

1 cup chopped nuts

Preheat oven to 350°. Melt margarine and brown sugar together in saucepan. Remove from heat when combined and stir in eggs one at time. Add flour, baking powder and salt gradually until well blended. Add vanilla and nuts. Spray 9 x 13 inch aluminum pan with baking spray. Bake for 20 to 25 minutes. Cool completely and cut into squares.

Yield: 24 to 32 squares

Apple Pound Cake

1½ cups cooking oil

2 cups sugar

3 eggs

3 cups all-purpose flour

1 teaspoon salt

1 teaspoon baking soda

1½ teaspoons vanilla

3 large apples, peeled and cut into small pieces

1 cup chopped pecans

SAUCE

½ cup (1 stick) butter

½ cup brown sugar

2 tablespoons milk

Preheat oven to 325°. Combine and beat oil, sugar and eggs for 3 minutes at medium speed. Add flour, salt, soda and vanilla and mix well. Fold in apples and nuts. Bake in well greased and floured 9 x 13 inch baking pan for 1 hour and 20 minutes. Cool for 10 minutes before adding sauce. Bring all sauce ingredients to boil. Reduce heat to low and cook for 20 minutes. Pour over cooled cake. Sauce will be thin and soak into cake.

Yield: 15 servings

Lime Cheesecake with Raspberry Sauce

2 cups ginger snap crumbs
2½ cups sugar, divided
½ cup (1 stick) butter or margarine, melted
4 (8-ounce) packages cream cheese, softened
6 eggs
1 tablespoon grated lime (or lemon) rind
½ cup lime (or lemon) juice
1⅛ teaspoons vanilla, divided
16 ounces sour cream
1 (10-ounce) box frozen raspberries

Preheat oven to 325°. Stir together crumbs, ¼ cup sugar and margarine. Press mixture into bottom and sides of lightly greased 10 inch springform pan. Chill for 1 hour. Beat cream cheese until smooth. Add eggs one at a time, beating well after each. Gradually add 1¾ cups sugar, beating until blended. Stir in lime rind, juice and 1 teaspoon vanilla. Pour mixture into crust. Bake for 1 hour or until center is almost set. Cool for 10 minutes. Stir together remaining ½ cup sugar, ⅛ teaspoon vanilla and sour cream. Spread evenly over cheesecake. Bake for 10 minutes. Cool for 1 hour. Cover and chill cheesecake for 10 hours. Process raspberries until smooth, stopping to scrape down sides. Press purée through strainer, discarding seeds. Serve raspberry sauce with cheesecake.

Yield: 16 slices

Crust Variations
Graham Cracker Crust

Mix together 1½ cups graham cracker crumbs, 3 tablespoons sugar and ⅓ cup melted butter or margarine

Chocolate Crust

Substitute chocolate graham crackers or finely crushed chocolate crème filled cookies, omitting sugar and reducing margarine to 2 tablespoons.

Cheesecake Variations
Cappuccino Cheesecake

Mix 3 tablespoons coffee-flavored liqueur (Kahlúa) and 1 tablespoon instant coffee until dissolved. Add to filling mixture. Use chocolate crust.

Chocolate Chip Cheesecake

Stir ¾ cup mini semi-sweet chocolate chips into filling mixture.

Cheesecake Variations continued

Chocolate Cheesecake

Mix in 4 squares melted semi-sweet chocolate, slightly cooled, to filling mixture.

Blueberry Cheesecake

Add ½ cup blueberries to filling mixture and sprinkle ½ cup blueberries on top.

Praline Cheesecake

Stir ½ cup almond brickle bits into filling mixture.

Company Coconut Cake

1	box white cake mix with pudding	½	teaspoon vanilla
¾	cup vegetable oil	3	eggs
		¾	cup cream of coconut

COCONUT CREAM CHEESE ICING

1	(8-ounce) package cream cheese	1	pound (16-ounce) box confectioners' sugar
½	cup (1 stick) butter or margarine, softened	1	(7-ounce) package flaked coconut
1	teaspoon vanilla		

Preheat oven to 325°. Mix together all ingredients for cake and divide into two 9 inch greased and floured, round cake pans. Bake for 45 minutes. Remove from oven and cool on racks. For icing, combine cream cheese, butter and vanilla. Mix until creamy. Add confectioners' sugar and blend until smooth. When cake layers are cooled, ice cake and sprinkle top and sides of cake with coconut.

Yield: 12 slices

Chocolate Molten Cakes

1 cup (2 sticks) unsalted butter	3 tablespoons sour cream
3 ounces unsweetened chocolate	1 teaspoon vanilla
2 cups sugar	1 (12-ounce) bag semi-sweet
1 cup all purpose flour	chocolate chips
Pinch salt	Vanilla ice cream as
3 large eggs	accompaniment

Preheat oven to 350°. In small saucepan, melt butter. Add unsweetened chocolate and melt. Whisk together sugar, flour and salt in mixing bowl. Whisk in melted butter mixture until combined. Whisk in eggs, sour cream and vanilla until well mixed. Stir in chocolate chips. Pour batter into 8 to 10 greased ramekins or 12 muffin tins sprayed with baking spray and place on baking sheet. Bake in middle of oven for 30 to 35 minutes or until almost set throughout. Can be made 1 day ahead and chilled, covered. Bring to room temperature and reheat in 350° oven until warm, about 5 minutes. Serve in ramekin or unmold. Good with raspberry sauce or sprinkle with confectioners' sugar. These are so rich and dense, the smaller size is preferable.

Yield: 8 to 12 servings

RASPBERRY SAUCE

1 (24-ounce) package frozen raspberries or strawberries	¼ teaspoon lemon juice
⅓ cup sugar	Pinch salt

Place frozen berries in large saucepan. Bring to simmer, stirring occasionally for 10 minutes. Add sugar and raise heat to high. Boil for 2 minutes. Strain berries over bowl and discard seeds. Cover and refrigerate for 2 hours before serving.

Yield: 2 cups

Note: Chocolate Molten Cake was actually a mistake! A chocolate sponge cake was taken from the oven before it was done with the center still runny. While still warm, it had both good taste and good texture. There is now a mix on the market for less ambitious cooks.

Aunt Lou's Crunch Cake

2	cups sugar	2	cups all-purpose flour
1	cup vegetable oil	¼	teaspoon salt
6	eggs	2	tablespoons vanilla

MAMA'S CARAMEL TOPPING

½	cup butter or margarine	1	teaspoon baking powder
2	cups brown sugar	1	teaspoon vanilla
5	tablespoons evaporated milk		

Preheat oven to 300°. For cake: using an electric mixer, cream sugar and oil. Add eggs two at a time and beat well. Combine salt and flour. Gradually add to mixture and continue beating. Add vanilla and mix well. Grease Bundt pan with non stick cooking spray and dust with flour. Cook for approximately 1 hour 15 minutes. Toothpick inserted in cake should come out clean. Top of cake should be crunchy when removed from oven. Let cake rest in pan until it will release. Cool on rack. For topping: cook butter, sugar and milk until mixture comes to boil. Boil for 2 minutes, stirring constantly. Add baking powder and vanilla. Topping will foam over and become thick. Beat until thick enough to pour over cake. Allow to cool and serve.

Yield: 16 slices

Ralph Newton's Pound Cake

3	cups all-purpose flour	1½	cups butter or margarine
3	cups sugar	1½	teaspoons lemon, vanilla or
9	eggs		almond extract

Preheat oven to 300°. Combine all ingredients in large bowl; blend well until smooth. Beat on medium speed of electric mixer 10 to 15 minutes or until very fluffy. Spoon batter into greased and floured 10 inch tube or Bundt pan. Bake for 1 hour 25 minutes or until toothpick inserted comes out clean. Cool for 30 minutes before removing from pan.

Yield: 16 slices

Historical Note: The original pound cake was so named because it contained one pound each of butter, sugar, eggs and flour. Since few people could read at this time, this was an easy recipe to remember.

Gooey Butter Cake

CRUST

1 package plain yellow cake mix

½ cup (1 stick) butter or
margarine, melted

1 large egg

FILLING

1 (8-ounce) package cream
cheese at room temperature

2 large eggs

1 teaspoon vanilla

½ cup (1 stick) butter or
margarine, melted

3¾ cups confectioners' sugar,
sifted

Preheat oven to 350°. For crust: place cake mix, melted butter and egg in mixing bowl. Blend with electric mixer on low speed for 2 minutes. Scrape down sides of bowl. Batter should come together in ball. Pat batter evenly into bottom ungreased 9 x 13 inch baking pan. Set aside. For filling: place cream cheese in same bowl used for crust and blend on low speed until fluffy, 30 seconds. Stop mixer: add eggs, vanilla and melted butter and beat for 1 minute. Stop mixer and add confectioners' sugar on medium until incorporated, about 1 minute. Pour filling onto crust and spread with spatula so filling covers entire surface. Place pan in oven on center rack and bake for 45 to 47 minutes or until well browned. Cool on wire rack.

Variations

Chocolate Marble Gooey Cake

Add 1 (6-ounce) package semisweet chocolate chips to filling.

Lemon Chess Gooey Cake

Add 2 teaspoons grated lemon zest, 6 tablespoons juice (from 2 lemons) and 2 tablespoons yellow cornmeal to filling.

Almond Gooey Cake

Add 1 teaspoon vanilla and ½ cup slivered almonds to crust.

Coconut-Pecan Gooey Cake

Add 1 cup finely chopped pecans and 1 cup frozen unsweetened grated coconut to crust.

Yield: 20 servings

Note: Gooey butter cakes are a cross between a sheet cake and a bar. They're so soft you'll need a fork to savor every bite, but they have the firm crust of a bar cookie.

Lemon Pound Cake with Lemon Glaze

1	cup (2 sticks) butter or margarine	3½	cups all-purpose flour
3	cups sugar	½	teaspoon baking powder
6	eggs	1	teaspoon salt
1	cup milk	1	teaspoon lemon extract
		1	teaspoon vanilla extract

GLAZE

	Juice of 1 lemon	1	teaspoon lemon rind
1	tablespoon butter or margarine	1½	cups confectioners' sugar

Preheat oven to 325°. Cream sugar and shortening. Add two eggs at time. Beat well after each addition. Sift flour and measure exactly 3½ cups. Add baking powder and salt to flour and sift again. Add milk and flour alternately, beating after each addition, starting with flour and ending with flour. Add flavorings and beat. Pour into greased and floured Bundt and bake for 1 hour 15 minutes or until wooden toothpick inserted in cake comes out clean. Cool for 10 minutes. Remove from pan. For glaze: mix all ingredients together. Pour over cake and drizzle down sides while cake is hot.

Yield: 12 to 16 pieces

Tennessee Cherry Crumble

2	cans cherry pie filling	½	cup chopped nuts
2	teaspoons lemon juice	½	cup (1 stick) butter or margarine, melted
1	package white deluxe cake mix		

Preheat oven to 350°. Spread pie filling on bottom 9 x 13 inch baking pan. Sprinkle with lemon juice. Combine dry cake mix, nuts and melted butter. Sprinkle crumbly mixture over pie filling and bake for 40 to 50 minutes until golden brown.

Yield: 24 squares

Tennessee Rum Cake

1	package yellow cake mix	½	cup rum
1	small package vanilla instant pudding	½	cup vegetable oil
		½	cup water
4	eggs	1	cup chopped pecans

TOPPING

½	cup butter	¼	cup rum
¼	cup water	1	cup sugar

Preheat oven to 350°. Beat together all ingredients except pecans and topping ingredients, adding eggs one at a time. Spray Bundt pan with non-stick baking spray and sprinkle with pecans. Pour batter on top of pecans and bake for 50 minutes or until inserted knife comes out clean. Boil topping ingredients for 3 minutes and pour directly onto hot cake. Let sit for 30 minutes and invert onto cake plate.

Yield: 16 slices

Variation
Kentucky Bourbon Cake

Substitute bourbon for rum.

Historical Note: Pecans are true blue-blood American since they were growing wild before any new-comers arrived in the U.S. and they don't grow naturally in any other part of the world. Georgia is the nation's largest supplier of pecans, with more than half of the total U.S. production.

Texas Sheet Cake

1 cup (2 sticks) butter or margarine
1 cup water
4 tablespoons cocoa
2 cups all-purpose flour

2 cups sugar
½ teaspoon salt
1 teaspoon baking soda
2 eggs
½ cup sour cream

FROSTING

½ cup (1 stick) butter or margarine
4 tablespoons cocoa
6 tablespoons milk

1 pound confectioners' sugar
1 teaspoon vanilla
1 cup pecan pieces

Preheat oven to 375°. Boil butter, water and cocoa in small saucepan; remove from heat. Combine flour, sugar, baking powder and salt. Beat in eggs, sour cream and cocoa mixture. Pour into 11 x 14 inch greased jelly-roll pan. Bake for 20 minutes. For frosting: boil butter, cocoa and milk in medium saucepan. Remove from heat. Stir in sugar, vanilla and pecans. Beat well. Spread over cake while still hot.

Yield: 60 squares

Bourbon Pecan Pie

¼ cup (½ stick) butter or margarine
1 cup brown sugar
3 eggs, beaten
¾ cup light corn syrup
1 teaspoon vanilla

¼ teaspoon salt
1 cup chopped pecans
2 tablespoons bourbon
1 (9 or 10-inch) frozen unbaked pie shell, defrosted
1 cup heavy cream, whipped

Preheat oven to 375°. Cream butter; beat in brown sugar slowly. Add eggs, corn syrup, vanilla and salt. Blend well. Stir in pecans and bourbon. Pour filling into pie shell and bake for 40 to 45 minutes. Serve topped with whipped cream.

Yield: 8 to 10 slices

Chocolate Pie

3 egg whites at room temperature

½ teaspoon cream of tarter

¾ cup sugar

½ teaspoon vanilla

¾ cup ice box chocolate wafer crumbs (about 13 wafers)

½ cup chopped pecans

Sweetened whipped cream

Preheat oven to 325°. Beat egg whites and cream of tarter until stiff; gradually add sugar. Add vanilla and fold in crumbs and nuts. Pour into well-greased pie pan. Bake for about 35 minutes. Allow to cool completely. Top with sweetened whipped cream.

Yield: 8 to 10 slices

French Silk Pie

3 egg whites (at room temperature)

⅛ teaspoon salt

¼ teaspoon cream of tartar

¾ cup sugar

½ cup chopped pecans

½ teaspoon vanilla extract

4 ounces sweet baking chocolate

3 tablespoons water

1 tablespoon brandy

2 cups whipping cream, divided

Shaved chocolate for garnish

Preheat oven to 300°. Beat egg whites with salt and cream of tartar until soft peaks form. Gradually add sugar and beat until stiff. Fold in nuts and vanilla. Pour into greased 9 inch pie pan, building up sides to form rim. Bake for 50 minutes. Cool. In top of double boiler, melt chocolate with water. Add brandy. Whip 1 cup cream and fold into chocolate mixture. Allow chocolate mixture to cool. Pile into meringue shell. Chill for at least 5 hours. Serve with dollop of whipped cream topped with shaved chocolate on each slice.

Yield: 8 slices

To fold beaten egg whites into batter more easily, mix one fourth into the heavier batter first. You lose some of the bubbles but the remaining egg whites will mix better due to the new consistency of the batter. Also, be sure to add the egg whites to the batter and not the reverse, as the heaviest ingredient must be on the bottom.

Key Lime Pie

1 (14-ounce) can Eagle Brand
   sweetened condensed milk
1 (8-ounce) package cream
   cheese, softened
¾ cup Key lime juice

½ teaspoon vanilla
   Graham cracker crust
    (prepared crust may be used)
   Whipped cream

Blend milk, cheese and juice until light and fluffy. Add vanilla. Pour into crust and refrigerate. Served topped with whipped cream. Thin lime slices make a nice garnish.

Yield: 8 slices

Lemon Chess Pie

2 cups sugar
2 tablespoons cornmeal
2 tablespoons all-purpose flour
   Grated lemon rind (optional)
5 eggs

½ cup melted butter or
   margarine
½ cup milk
½-⅔ cup lemon juice
2 (9-inch) unbaked pie shells

Preheat oven to 350°. Mix sugar, cornmeal, flour, and lemon rind. Add eggs, butter, milk and lemon juice and mix well. Pour into unbaked pie shells and bake for 35 to 45 minutes until filling is lightly browned and firm. (When using premade, frozen pie shells in thin aluminum pans, invert cast iron skillets in the oven and bake pies on top of these for a lightly browned, flaky crust.)

Yield: 2 pies; 8 slices per pie

Historical Note: Chess Pies have been a favorite in southern homes for many years. One legend of the origin of the name maintains that, when asked what was for dessert, the cook replied, "It's chus' pie". This meant she had "just" used ingredients on hand, such as eggs, butter, sugar and any flavorings that might be available.

Strawberry Glazed Pie

1 baked pie shell	5 tablespoons cornstarch
1⅓ cups water	1 cup heavy cream
1 quart fresh strawberries	1 tablespoon confectioners' sugar
1 cup sugar	Sprinkling of nutmeg

Wash and hull strawberries. Mix 1 cup strawberries, 1 cup water and sugar together. Bring to boil quickly; then reduce heat and cook gently for 15 minutes. Add several drops red food coloring if desired. Mix cornstarch and remaining water to form paste. Add to cooked strawberries. Cook over low heat, stirring constantly until thick. Beat cream until stiff peaks are formed. Stir in confectioners' sugar. Spread half whipped cream mixture in bottom of baked pie shell. Sprinkle with nutmeg. Put 3 cups hulled strawberries on top of whipped cream. Top with cooled strawberry glaze. Chill about 3 hours. Just before serving, dot remaining whipped cream over top of pie.

Yield: 8 to 10 slices

Variation
Peach or Blueberry Glazed Pie

Peaches or Blueberries may be substituted for strawberries.

Toffee Squares

1 cup butter or margarine	2 cups all-purpose flour
1 cup brown sugar, packed	1 (12-ounce) package semi-sweet chocolate chips
1 egg yolk	
1 teaspoon vanilla	½ cup finely chopped nuts

Preheat oven to 350°. Cream butter, sugar, egg yolk and vanilla. Stir in flour and pat into 10 x 13 inch rectangle on greased baking sheet. (Or for easier removal, use parchment paper on sheet). Be sure to leave 1 inch around edges because dough spreads as it bakes. Bake 20 to 25 minutes. Remove from oven and immediately put chips on top of hot cookie. Let stand until soft enough to spread evenly over top. Sprinkle with nuts and cut into small squares.

Yield: 5 to 6 dozen squares

Boiled Custard

4	eggs	4	cups milk
1	cup sugar	1	teaspoon vanilla

Beat eggs and sugar. Add milk. Place in top of double boiler and cook until thick, stirring occasionally. Strain and chill. Before serving, stir in vanilla.

Yield: 6 to 8 servings

Variation
Floating Island Pudding

Preheat oven to 350°. Substitute 2 whole eggs plus 2 egg yolks for 4 eggs in custard recipe. Reserve whites. Grease six 5 ounce custard cups; sprinkle with sugar to coat. Beat reserved egg whites and ⅛ teaspoon cream of tartar until foamy. Beat in ¼ cup sugar, 1 tablespoon at a time. Continue beating until stiff and glossy. Spoon meringue into cups, pressing mixture gently into cups to remove air pockets. Place cups in baking pan. Pour in very hot water (1 inch deep). Bake for 20 to 25 minutes or until lightly browned. Remove cups from water and unmold into dessert dishes. Cool slightly and chill. Just before serving, spoon above custard around meringue.

Yield: 6 servings

Variation
Savannah Trifle

1	loaf pound cake, cut in 1 inch cubes or 2 dozen ladyfingers	½	cup (or more to taste) cream sherry, whiskey or rum
		1½-2	cups heavy cream, whipped

Sprinkle pound cake with sherry and let absorb. Place half cake in glass serving bowl. Pour half above custard over cake. Spread half whipped cream over custard. Repeat and chill.

Yield: 10 to 12 servings

Eggs separate best when cold, but egg whites need to be at room temperature for greater volume when whipped. (When baking, all ingredients should be at room temperature for best results.)

Classic Crème Brûlée

8   egg yolks (save whites for
    Chocolate Chewies)
⅓   cup sugar
2   cups heavy cream

1   teaspoon pure vanilla
¼   cup brown sugar
    (for caramelized top)

Preheat oven to 350°. Beat egg yolks and sugar together until sugar is dissolved and mixture is thick and pale yellow. Add cream and vanilla; mix until well blended. Strain into large bowl, skimming off any foam or bubbles. Divide mixture between 6 ramekins or custard cups. Place ramekins in pan, carefully filling pan with hot water until level reaches halfway up sides of ramekins. Bake until set around edges but still soft in center, about 40 to 50 minutes. Longer baking time will be required for larger, deeper ramekins. Remove from oven and leave in water bath until cooled. Remove and chill for at least 2 hours or up to 2 days. When ready to serve, sift about 2 teaspoons brown sugar over each ramekin. Place under broiler until sugar melts. Re-chill custards for few minutes before serving by placing ramekins on bed of ice.

Yield: 6 servings

Variations
Blueberry Crème Brûlée

Divide ⅓ to ½ cup blueberries in bottom of ramekins, pour crème over and bake.

Cappuccino Crème Brûlée

Add 2 teaspoons instant espresso powder, 1 teaspoon cinnamon and ⅛ teaspoon nutmeg to crème while heating.

Irish Cream Crème Brûlée

Add 3 tablespoons good-quality Irish Cream to crème.

Kahlúa Crème Brûlée

Add ¼ cup Kahlúa plus ¼ teaspoon instant espresso powder to crème.

Amaretto Crème Brûlée

Mix 3 tablespoons amaretto plus ⅛ teaspoon almond extract into crème.
Note: Crème brûlée, the French term for a rich baked custard, is more appealing than its English name, burnt cream.

Chocolate Éclair Dessert

2 (3-ounce) packages instant
   vanilla pudding
3 cups whole milk

1 (8-ounce) carton Cool Whip
1 (16-ounce) box graham
   crackers

FROSTING

2 tablespoons butter or
   margarine
2 squares semi-sweet chocolate

2 tablespoons milk
2 tablespoons white corn syrup
½ cup confectioners' sugar

Prepare pudding according to package directions, using 3 cups of milk. Fold in Cool Whip. Cover bottom of 9 x 13 inch pan with graham crackers. Place half pudding mixture over crackers. Repeat layers, ending with crackers. Prepare frosting: melt butter and chocolate over low heat in small saucepan. Gradually add milk and corn syrup. Beat in confectioners' sugar until smooth. Should resemble medium chocolate sauce more than thickened frosting. Pour over top layer of graham crackers. Refrigerate overnight.

Yield: 24 squares

Debbie's Famous Pralines

3 tablespoons butter or
   margarine
½ cup light brown sugar, firmly
   packed
1 cup granulated sugar

½ cup evaporated milk
1½ teaspoons light corn syrup
⅛ teaspoon salt
1 teaspoon vanilla extract
1 cup pecan pieces

Melt butter over medium heat in heavy saucepan. Add sugars, milk, corn syrup and salt, stirring until well blended. Continue cooking and stirring until mixture reaches 246° on candy thermometer or medium firm ball forms when small amount is dropped in cup of tap water. Remove from heat and let stand for 2 to 3 minutes. Stir in vanilla and pecans. Using 2 spoons, drop the mixture onto wax paper. Make your pralines any size desired! Let cool and enjoy!

Yield: 2 dozen medium

Easy Tiramisu

1 (28-ounce) package milk
   or dark chocolate Nestle
   European Style Mousse Mix

⅔ cup milk

1 (8-ounce) package mascarpone
   cheese

1 cup strong brewed coffee or
   espresso, cooled to room
   temperature

3 tablespoons brandy or Kahlúa

2 (3½-ounce) packages
   ladyfingers, divided

   Shaved chocolate

Prepare mousse mix according to steps 1 and 2 of package directions, using ⅔ cup milk. Fold mascarpone cheese into prepared mousse. Combine coffee and brandy in small bowl. Line bottom of 8 inch square baking dish with half ladyfingers; drizzle with half coffee mixture. Spoon half mousse mixture over ladyfingers; top with remaining lady fingers. Drizzle with remaining coffee mixture. Spoon remaining mousse mixture over ladyfingers. Sprinkle with chocolate. Refrigerate for 2 hours before serving.

Yield: 8 servings

Historical Note: Tiramisu, first created in Siena, Italy, was a favorite of Venetians. The literal translation of "tirami-su" is "pick-me-up" and with the strong espresso coffee it contains, it is aptly named.

Heavenly Hot Fudge Sauce

4 squares unsweetened chocolate

½ cup butter or margarine

   Dash salt

3 cups sugar

1 (12-ounce) can evaporated
   milk, heated

1 teaspoon vanilla

Melt chocolate and butter in top of double boiler. Add salt and stir. Add sugar slowly, followed by milk. Stir until well mixed. Remove from heat and add vanilla.

Yield: 1 quart

Motor Home Marvel

12-18 ice cream sandwiches
1 (12¼-ounce) jar Smucker's Caramel Sauce
1 (12-ounce) container Cool Whip
1 (8-ounce) package Heath Bar Brickle Bits

Wedge unwrapped ice cream sandwiches in 9 x 13 inch pan. Punch holes in sandwiches with big fork. Pour Smucker's caramel sauce over top. Spread Cool Whip over sauce and sprinkle with Heath Bar Brickle Bits. Freeze.

Yield: 24 squares

Note: So named because it can be made in back of moving vehicle. A very "kid friendly" dessert!

Sarah's Mud Pie Squares

1 (15-ounce) package Oreo cookies
½ cup (1 stick) butter or margarine, softened plus 6 tablespoons
½ gallon coffee ice cream
3 teaspoons almond flavoring, divided
1 cup sugar
1 (5-ounce) can evaporated milk
4 squares semi-sweet chocolate
1 (12-ounce) container Cool Whip
1 cup chopped nuts

Crush Oreos and mix with 1 stick softened margarine. Press into 9 x 13 inch pan. Soften ice cream and mix in 1 teaspoon almond flavoring. Spread over Oreo mixture and freeze. Boil sugar, milk, 1 teaspoon almond flavoring, chocolate and 6 tablespoons margarine for 1 minute. Cool well, place on top of ice cream and freeze. Mix Cool Whip, nuts and 1 teaspoon almond flavoring. Spread on top and freeze. Take out just before serving and cut into squares.

Yield: 24 squares

Swedish Crème Dessert

1 envelope Knox gelatin	2 cups sour cream
2 cups whipping cream	1 teaspoon vanilla
1 cup sugar	

Dissolve gelatin in ½ cup cold whipping cream. Mix remaining whipping cream, sugar and dissolved gelatin mixture. Set over low heat until gelatin completely dissolves. Cool until slightly thickened. Carefully fold in sour cream and vanilla. Blend well. Turn into custard cups, sherbet glasses or mold, sprayed with cooking spray to make unmolding easier. Refrigerate overnight. Serve with raspberries or similar fruit or sauce. Can be prepared a week in advance.

Yield: 10 servings

Note: To fold one mixture into another, mix one fourth into the heavier batter first. You lose some of the bubbles but the remaining mixture will mix better due to the new consistency of the batter. Also, be sure to add the lighter and not the reverse, as the heaviest ingredients must be on the bottom.

Vera's Pudim de Larjanja
(Easy Orange Flan)

1¼ cups sugar, divided	15 ounces orange juice
3 eggs plus 2 yolks	(fresh squeezed preferred)
1 (15-ounce) can sweetened condensed milk	

Preheat oven to 375°. Caramelize Bundt pan with 1 cup sugar. Place sugar in heavy saucepan over medium to high heat, stirring constantly for about 5 minutes. Sugar will begin to brown and liquefy in pan. Lower heat if necessary so sugar does not burn. When sugar is completely melted and browned, add to Bundt pan. Tilt pan so sugar is evenly distributed. Cool pan in cold water. (It will set immediately and crackle.) Mix eggs and yolks, sweetened condensed milk, orange juice and ¼ cup sugar in blender. Pour into caramelized pan and place in bain-marie or water bath (2 inches hot water in baking pan). Bake for 1 hour. Let cool until ready to serve. Invert Bundt pan onto serving dish. The caramelized sugar will have again melted and will be sauce over flan. If too much sauce, remove some before serving. Can be served with dollop whipped cream, an orange slice or chocolate-orange stick.

Yield: 6 servings

Note: This recipe came from Brazil. It is one of the country's favorite traditional desserts.

⇻ INDEX ⇺

❧ Index ❧

❧ INDEX ❧

Cereals and Grains

Cheese

❖ Index ❖

❋ INDEX ❋

❧ Index ❧

❧ Index ❧

❧ INDEX ❧

Moss, Marshes & Memorable Meals
Mail to: Isle of Hope United Methodist Women
412 Parkersburg Road
Savannah, GA 31406

Please send ____copies of
 Moss, Marshes & Memorable Meals   @ $21.95 each $ _____

Add postage and handling for first book   @ $ 4.50 each $ _____

For each additional book to same address @ $ 3.00 each $ _____

            TOTAL _____

Ship To:
Name _____

Address_____

City _____ State _____ ZIP _____

Please make checks payable to:
Isle of Hope United Methodist Women

Moss, Marshes & Memorable Meals
Mail to: Isle of Hope United Methodist Women
412 Parkersburg Road
Savannah, GA 31406

Please send ____copies of
 Moss, Marshes & Memorable Meals   @ $21.95 each $ _____

Add postage and handling for first book   @ $ 4.50 each $ _____

For each additional book to same address @ $ 3.00 each $ _____

            TOTAL _____

Ship To:
Name _____

Address_____

City _____ State _____ ZIP _____

Please make checks payable to:
Isle of Hope United Methodist Women

Moss, Marshes & Memorable Meals
Mail to: Isle of Hope United Methodist Women
412 Parkersburg Road
Savannah, GA 31406

Please send _____copies of
    Moss, Marshes & Memorable Meals @ $21.95 each $ _____

Add postage and handling for first book @ $ 4.50 each $ _____

For each additional book to same address @ $ 3.00 each $ _____

                                                     TOTAL _____

Ship To:
Name _____

Address_____

City _____ State _____ ZIP _____

Please make checks payable to:
Isle of Hope United Methodist Women

Moss, Marshes & Memorable Meals
Mail to: Isle of Hope United Methodist Women
412 Parkersburg Road
Savannah, GA 31406

Please send _____copies of
    Moss, Marshes & Memorable Meals @ $21.95 each $ _____

Add postage and handling for first book @ $ 4.50 each $ _____

For each additional book to same address @ $ 3.00 each $ _____

                                                     TOTAL _____

Ship To:
Name _____

Address_____

City _____ State _____ ZIP _____

Please make checks payable to:
Isle of Hope United Methodist Women